商务对话
口译实战

主 编 曾思予
副主编 姚 琦 文佩玲 赖丽伟

Business Dialogue
Interpreting

清华大学出版社
北京

内 容 简 介

本教材注重理论与实战结合，每单元从一个口译理论或口译技巧出发，重点培养学生基础口译知识和技能。本书还特别关注实战练习，为学生提供了丰富多样的练习材料，其中包括与理论知识匹配的句子或段落练习及讲解和课后篇章口译练习、对话口译练习等。本书每个单元配套音频资源，读者可先扫描封底的"文泉云盘防盗码"解锁资源后，再扫描书中对应处的二维码获取听力资源。

本书使用对象主要是高等院校的商务口译专业的本科生，也适合对英语口译或笔译感兴趣的读者自学使用。

版权所有，侵权必究。举报：010-62782989，beiqinquan@tup.tsinghua.edu.cn。

图书在版编目（CIP）数据

商务对话口译实战 / 曾思予主编 . -- 北京：清华大学出版社, 2024.7. --ISBN 978-7-302-66714-8

I. F7

中国国家版本馆 CIP 数据核字第 2024JX7426 号

责任编辑：徐博文
封面设计：李伯骥
责任校对：王荣静
责任印制：刘海龙

出版发行：清华大学出版社
    网　　址：https://www.tup.com.cn, https://www.wqxuetang.com
    地　　址：北京清华大学学研大厦 A 座　邮　编：100084
    社 总 机：010-83470000　邮　购：010-62786544
    投稿与读者服务：010-62776969, c-service@tup.tsinghua.edu.cn
    质量反馈：010-62772015, zhiliang@tup.tsinghua.edu.cn
印 装 者：河北鹏润印刷有限公司
经　　销：全国新华书店
开　　本：170mm×230mm　印　张：12.25　字　数：202 千字
版　　次：2024 年 9 月第 1 版　印　次：2024 年 9 月第 1 次印刷
定　　价：62.00 元

产品编号：104452-01

在这个充满变化和机遇的全球化时代，商务交流与合作已成为连接世界的桥梁。尽管人工智能发展迅猛，人与人之间的交际需求还是不可替代的。口译员作为跨越语言障碍的连接者，在促进国际商务交流和理解方面扮演着重要的角色。如今，商务英语、国际商务等专业仍然是高考学子较热门的志愿选择，该类专业的学生应具有扎实的英语语言技能和基本的商务知识。针对商务领域的口译学习对他们的语言能力和商务专业水平将具有积极的作用，而商务口译领域最广泛的形式是对话口译，这是众多口译学习者初入市场实践时常见的口译形式。

市场上现有的商务英语对话口译的相关教材相对较少，且部分难度较高，不适合口译初学者。本教材内容丰富、实用且切合实际，适合对商务对话口译感兴趣的学生，如英语专业、商务英语专业的口译初学者；国际商务、国际贸易等非语言类专业但希望通过学习口译提高语言能力并提高商务技能的学生；需要在商务环境中从事口译工作、希望通过系统学习和实战练习提高商务对话口译水平的职场人士。

本教材注重理论与实战结合，每单元从一种口译理论或口译技巧出发，重点培养学生基础口译知识和技能。同时，本教材特别关注实战练习，为读者提供了丰富多样的练习材料，其中包括与理论知识匹配的句子或段落练习及讲解、课后篇章口译练习、对话口译练习等。本教材的对话口译练习改编自深圳技术大学商学院2021级国际商务专业的学生在商务英语课堂上的小组展示。通过本教材的口译练习，读者将能够逐步提高听力和口译的能力，熟练掌握商务对话的表达技巧，并更好地应对现实工作中的挑战。本教材还与多媒体技术紧密结合，为读者提供配套的音频素材。通过扫码，读者可以直接跟听原文进行练习，进一步加强听力和口译的能力。我们相信，多媒体的辅助将为读者提供更加便捷高效的体验。

衷心感谢清华大学出版社的大力支持，希望本教材能够成为读者在学习中的得力助手，帮助读者了解基本商务知识，全面提高英语交际能力，进而在全球化的舞台上展现出更加卓越的口译技能和综合素养。祝读者在学习和实践中获得丰富的收获！由于编者水平有限，书中难免有疏漏和不足之处，恳请广大读者和同人提出宝贵意见，以便再版时进行修正。

编写组

2024 年 5 月

第 1 单元　口译导论 1

1.1　什么是口译 2
1.2　口译的分类 2
1.3　口译的标准 3
1.4　口译的过程 5
1.5　口译训练法 6
1.6　口译练习 7
1.7　练习原文及解析 7

第 2 单元　记忆训练 9

2.1　记忆训练的重要性 10
2.2　记忆的工作机制 10
2.3　记忆策略 11
2.4　记忆训练方法 12
2.5　口译练习 14
2.6　练习原文、译文及解析 16

第 3 单元　口译笔记法 37

3.1　口译笔记的特征 38
3.2　口译笔记的内容 39
3.3　口译笔记的方法 39
3.4　口译练习 43
3.5　练习原文、译文及解析 45

第 4 单元　数字口译 71

4.1　英汉数字表达差异 72
4.2　数字的笔记及双语转换 74
4.3　倍数的翻译 74
4.4　口译练习 76
4.5　练习原文、译文及解析 79

第 5 单元　增译与减译 97

5.1　增译法 98
5.2　减译法 99
5.3　口译练习 100
5.4　练习原文、译文及解析 103

第 6 单元　视译 121

6.1　视译准备步骤 122
6.2　视译原则 122
6.3　视译练习技巧 123

6.4	口译练习	125
6.5	练习原文、译文及解析	131

第 7 单元　直译与意译 **145**

7.1	直译与意译	146
7.2	直译的运用	147
7.3	意译的运用	148
7.4	口译练习	149
7.5	练习原文、译文及解析	151

第 8 单元　公众演讲 **167**

8.1	如何做好公众演讲	168
8.2	公众演讲口译	170
8.3	口译练习	171
8.4	练习原文、译文	174

UNIT 1

第1单元

口译导论

在本单元中，我们将深入了解口译的基本概念、分类、相关标准以及整个口译过程，同时，我们将为大家介绍几种有效的口译练习方式。作为一种特殊的翻译形式，口译具有挑战性，它对口译员的听力、记忆和表达能力有较高要求。通过本单元的学习，你将全面认识口译，为日后的学习和实践奠定坚实的基础。

1.1 什么是口译

口译（interpreting）是一种跨语言和跨文化交际的艺术，它要求口译员在源语发出时，立刻转译为目的语，以确保实时的双向沟通。不同于笔译，口译作为一种实时性的翻译形式，要求口译员具有敏捷的反应能力和准确的表达能力；它不允许口译员回顾或更正已传递的内容，因此被形象地称为"一次性的演出"（one-time presentation）[1]。

1.2 口译的分类

根据工作模式，口译可以分为三种主要形式（图1-1）：

工作模式分类	
	交替传译（Consecutive interpreting）：交替传译是最传统的口译形式，口译员在一段源语发言结束后立刻进行翻译，将目的语内容传达给听众，翻译结束后，说话人开始下一段发言。这种形式适用于小规模会议、新闻发布会、商务洽谈等。
	同声传译（Simultaneous interpreting）：同声传译是口译员通过专业的同传设备，在听到源语内容时，立即通过耳机将目的语内容传达给听众。这种形式广泛应用于大型国际会议、高级别政府会议等，需要口译员具备高度的听力、记忆和表达能力。
	耳语传译（Whispering interpreting）：耳语传译是在口译员与受话人之间进行的。口译员一般位于受话人侧后方，将口译内容以轻声耳语传递给受话人。当一方语言使用者仅为一两人，且需节省时间时，常用耳语传译。它既不需像交传一样花费额外一倍甚至更多的时间给翻译，也不需要昂贵的同传设备。

图1-1 根据工作模式分类

---

[1] Pöchhacker, F. 2004. *Introducing Interpreting Studies*. New York: Routlegde.

此外，口译还可以根据译语方向进行分类，包括单向口译（从一种语言到另一种语言）和双向口译（在两种语言之间进行双向口译）。在实际口译场合选择单向口译还是双向口译，要综合考虑聘请口译员的人工成本、口译场合需要等。显然，对于口译学习者来说，熟练掌握双向口译技能是至关重要的。

口译涵盖多个领域，根据工作场合可分为多种口译形式，如商务口译、会议口译、展览口译、外事口译、军事口译、法务/法庭口译、社区口译、医学口译、导游口译、技术口译、联络/陪同口译、媒体口译等。每种场合都对口译员的专业能力和背景知识有具体的要求。在口译界我们常说，一名口译员要"know everything about something and something about everything"，即汲取各方面知识，同时如果可以专才于某一领域（也许是本身具备该领域的专业知识，抑或是通过某次口译活动充分地进行译前准备），那必定能在该领域的口译中做得十分出色。

在国际商务领域，商务对话口译是最常见的口译形式之一，用词通常较为专业和正式，且涵盖广泛的行业知识。口译员在掌握口译技能的同时，还要熟悉商务领域的常用行话、术语、缩略语、习惯表达、数字翻译等知识。

1.3 口译的标准

在进行口译工作时，我们需要遵循一定的标准，以确保翻译的准确性。不同的学者和口译专家提出了不同的标准，其中一些常见的标准包括：

1.3.1 国际会议口译译员协会（AIIC）评判口译质量的标准依据

AIIC 作为全球范围最广、最具专业性的会议口译译员协会，对广大译员具有重大指导意义。会议口译研究专家 Bühler 在 1986 年针对包含 AIIC 会员在内的问卷调查中[1]指出，评判口译质量的标准依据主要包括以下九项，既有语言层面标准也有非语言层面标准：

> 1. 与源语信息意思一致 Sense consistency with original message

---

[1] Bühler, H. 1986. Linguistic (semantic) and extralinguistic (pragmatic) criteria for the evaluation of conference interpretation and interpreters. *MULTILINGUA*, 5(4): 231–235.

2. 产出在逻辑上具有连贯性 Logical cohesion of utterance
3. 专业术语使用正确 Use of correct terminology
4. 信息完整 Completeness of interpretation
5. 表达流畅 Fluency of delivery
6. 无语法错误 Correct grammatical usage
7. 发音地道 Native accent
8. 声音悦耳 Pleasant voice
9. 风格恰当 Appropriate style

1.3.2 准确、通顺、及时[1]

这个标准强调口译的准确性、流畅性以及实时性，即口译员需要在源语讲话进行时，及时地进行目的语表达，保持信息的完整和连贯。所谓及时，从交替传译的角度来说，一般在讲者停止发言的三秒钟之内，译员应马上开始翻译；而对同声传译（包括耳语传译）来说，译员不可能做到与讲者发言完全同步，而要与讲者发言维持一定的距离，称为"听译时间差"（Ear Voice Span, EVS）。译员需要在长期的练习中找到合适的听译时间差。

1.3.3 全面、准确、通畅[2]

"全面"指信息内容、源语涵义全面；"准确"指内涵、术语、数字等转换准确；"通畅"指译语产出流畅，以及语音、语调、语气等副语言信息通达。

1.3.4 准、整、顺、快[3]

王斌华教授将口译标准阐述得更加具体，强调了口译应做到准确、完整、流畅和迅速。

总体来说，口译员应当全面准确地理解源语，并及时、流畅地用目的语传达讲者完整的发言。在商务对话场合更加要求口译准确达意，口译员要结合讲者的

---

1 李越然. 1999. 论口译的社会功能——口译理论基础初探. 中国翻译，(3): 9.

2 鲍刚. 2005. 口译理论概述. 北京：中国对外翻译出版公司.

3 王斌华. 2006. 口译：理论·技巧·实践. 武汉：武汉大学出版社.

言语和肢体语言来理解讲者的真正意思和目的，并用准确、简洁、清晰明确的词句和合适的语调来传达。当然，在实际口译工作中会有增译减译、直译意译等情况以更好地达成交流的目的，而非简单的"完整""全面"；我们将在之后的单元具体介绍更多的口译技巧。

1.4 口译的过程

口译是一个快速而复杂的过程，涉及多个环节，需要口译员协调配合，以确保翻译的准确性和连贯性。口译通常包括听、记、思、表[1]四个过程（图1-2）。

听 Listening	记 Memorizing	思 Processing	表 Delivering
口译员需要专心聆听源语讲话内容，确保准确理解信息。良好的听力是口译成功的基础。很多口译初学者的第一道难关就是听力。特别是英译汉练习时，常常因为听得一知半解而无法正确翻译。	在听取源语内容的同时，口译员需要迅速记忆所听到的内容，为后续的表达做准备。记忆分为短期记忆和长期记忆，同时口译员还可以通过口译笔记辅助记忆。	在记忆内容的基础上，口译员需要对信息进行加工处理，包括理解语境、捋清逻辑关系、辨别语义和词汇的多义性等。这一步骤是口译的核心，决定了口译的准确性和流畅性。	最后，口译员将处理好的信息用流利自然的目的语表达出来，使听众能够准确理解源语讲话内容。有时口译学习者发现，即使自己全听懂了，也都记下来了，到张口却说得磕磕绊绊。这需要口译员加强公众演讲以及双语文本的学习，储备表达。

图1-2 口译的过程

需要注意的是，以上四个步骤并非单向独立发生，而是同一时间内交叉进行的。这意味着口译员要具备多任务处理的技能，在短时间内同时完成多项高强度的任务。

---

1 胡庚申. 1993. 怎样学习当好译员. 合肥：中国科技大学出版社.

1.5 口译训练法

根据口译学习者的学习进阶,口译训练会经历不同的阶段。不同的口译训练方式可以帮助口译员逐步提高听力、记忆和表达能力,培养口译技巧。以下简单介绍从易到难的几个口译练习方式,本书的其他单元也将进一步阐述这些练习方式。

1.5.1 源语复述

听取源语内容后,用源语进行复述,检查是否准确复述源语信息。这种练习可以帮助口译员锻炼记忆和表达能力。源语片段(segment)的时长可以从 30 秒、1 分钟开始,逐步由短到长增加难度。要尽可能地还原源语内容,但并不是逐字逐句、一字不落地复述,而是要将源语内容的意义实质传达出来。

1.5.2 无笔记交传

听取源语内容后,不使用笔记直接进行口译。无笔记交传在商务访问、企业参观等场景下是非常常见的口译方式;因为在这些场合下,讲者及口译员往往不会固定坐在座位上,这导致笔记不便;且语段较短,一般也不需要笔记的辅助。口译学习者可以在源语复述的基础上加大难度,尝试无笔记交传。第二单元将深入探讨源语复述和无笔记交传,并介绍更为翔实的记忆策略。

1.5.3 口译笔记法

掌握有效的口译笔记技巧,帮助记忆和加工信息。口译笔记法有助于提高口译员的准确性和流畅性。更多口译笔记技巧将在第三单元呈现。

1.5.4 影子练习

影子练习(shadowing),即像影子一样跟读源语,旨在通过模仿提高流利度,同时提升信息听辨、信息存储、信息加工等能力。影子跟读并不要求像机器般完美复制源语;若某部分听不清,也不应敷衍了事。建议录下自己跟读的音频,并进行转写(transcribe),以核实跟读的完整性与流畅度。

1.6 口译练习

请首先尝试对以下两段材料进行源语复述。记录你的复述内容，并与原文进行比对，以确定遗漏的信息点。你也可以尝试无笔记交传、有笔记交传及影子练习。

Text 1

Text 2

1.7 练习原文及解析

Text 1

原文：

今天晚上，感谢在座的各位贵宾在百忙中抽空参加我们的展览会和晚宴。在这里，我要特别感谢展览会的10个支持单位。有赖各个支持单位，我们才可以把展览会办得那么细致而出色。正因你们的大力支持和推广，我们才能够为照明行业打造一个真正的国际商贸平台，将各方资源和智慧汇聚在这里。在这里，我们共同见证了照明行业的创新和发展，感受到了行业的蓬勃活力。展望未来，我们对下一届的展会充满信心和期待。我们将进一步扩大展会的规模，引入更多的国际合作伙伴，打造更具影响力的平台。同时，我们也将举办涵盖多个专题的照明论坛，为行业同仁提供更多的学习和交流机会。我相信，通过我们的共同努力，未来的照明行业将呈现更加灿烂的光芒。最后，我要再次感谢你们的光临，祝愿大家在本次展会中获得丰富的收获，度过一个愉快的晚上。让我们携手前行，共同见证照明行业的美好未来！谢谢！

（改编自广州光亚法兰克福展览公司总经理在2008广州国际照明展开幕晚宴上的欢迎辞）

练习解析：

本篇为经典的欢迎辞，在听力的过程中可以将演讲分成四大模块：欢迎及感谢—成就—展望未来—再次感谢。在记忆力最大限度内在各个模块中填充更加具体的信息。

Text 2

原文：

As we celebrate World Information Society Day, we extend an invitation to all our partners, as well as international organizations, non-governmental organizations and policy-makers, to support children and young people around the world in accessing ICT. This is critical for young people as it serves as a way for them to learn, to share information and knowledge, to improve their health and nutrition, and to communicate with their peers.

The key to achieving the world's development goals lies in investing in the future generation, especially by improving access to communication for today's children and enhancing their capacities.

* ICT: Information and Communication Technology 信息与通信技术

(Adapted from the message from Dr Hamadoun Touré, ITU Secretary-General on the World Information Society Day)

练习解析：

本文可拆解为三大模块：（1）WHO—邀请了什么人来参会；（2）WHY—为什么举办此次活动；（3）HOW—如何实现世界发展目标。

小贴士

建议找一位一起练习口译的小伙伴，两人既可互为讲者和译员，也可共同进行口译练习，互相提出练习过程中出现的问题。同伴互评（peer evaluation）在口译练习过程中也是非常重要的一环。希望本单元的学习能够为你打下坚实的口译基础，引领你进入更高层次的口译实战。让我们一起踏上口译之旅，探索这个精彩而充满挑战的领域吧！

UNIT 2
第 2 单元

记忆训练

在第 1 单元口译导论中，我们强调了"记"是口译过程中非常重要的一环。作为口译学习者，应如何进行记忆训练，有哪些记忆策略能辅助我们完成翻译任务？在本单元，我们将深入探索记忆训练的方法和技巧。

2.1 记忆训练的重要性

口译，作为一种严格受时间限制的高强度信息处理活动，需要依赖译员的记忆系统来完成信息的接收、处理、存储、提取、输出等工作[1]。在商务对话中，译员常常无法做笔记，故口译对记忆能力的依赖尤为显著。为增强此能力，译员需进行有意识的记忆训练，优化记忆策略，提高效率。

2.2 记忆的工作机制

认知科学家阿特金森（Atkinson）和希夫林（Shiffrin）[2]将人脑记忆系统划分为感官记忆、短期记忆、长期记忆三个子系统。译员首先通过听觉或视觉来接收源语信息，即形成感官记忆；对收到的源语信息进行加工处理和短暂储存，即形成短期记忆。一般短期记忆的信息经过充分、有深度的加工，比如复述、复习后，可转入长期记忆。长期记忆包括头脑长期存储的知识、经验、程序等信息。译员要调动长期记忆的信息来理解源语意义，从而顺利进行短期记忆的信息加工[3]。商务环境下的译员尤需重视短期记忆，因此口译的记忆训练主要着眼于提升。

---

1 任文，胡敏霞. 2010. 交替传译记忆机制的认知分析与记忆力训练策略. 译苑新谭，(1): 14.

2 Atkinson, R. C. & Shiffrin, R. M. 1968. Human memory: A proposed system and its control processes. *Psychology of Learning and Motivation*, 2: 89–195.

3 任文，胡敏霞. 2010. 交替传译记忆机制的认知分析与记忆力训练策略. 译苑新谭，(1): 14.

2.3 记忆策略

2.3.1 信息逻辑化

通常逻辑清晰、结构紧凑的内容会更容易记忆。然而，在口译实践中，译员常遭遇信息量大的长句或不连贯的表述。此时，译员需借助逻辑推理，辨明信息重点，进而进行信息重组。要锻炼信息逻辑化，译员应练就高度概括信息的能力，从整体把握语篇的结构和层级，抓住主题句、关键词或观点性内容[1]。

练习 1

请听录音，录音结束后请用源语复述。

2.3.2 信息视觉化

贴近生活、生动形象的描述也更容易记忆。双码记忆理论[2]认为，输入大脑的信息如果采用语言和图像两种方式进行编码，会比只用语言编码记忆得更牢。应用在口译记忆训练中，就是不仅要多听，还要多看各种文字和图像材料，锻炼联想能力。在口译过程中，如果听到的内容能够在脑海中视觉化（visualize）或者成为一个场景、一幅图像的话，则会加深译员的短期记忆。

练习 2

请听录音，录音结束后请用源语复述。

2.3.3 信息组块化

短时记忆的容量很有限，一般由 7±2 个信息单位构成，而每个信息单位可大可小。组块化记忆就是将一些零散的、各自独立的短小信息单位，用逻辑分析、归纳整理、找共同规律等方式串联起来，归入一个或几个大的信息组块，从而减

---

1 高璐夷，储常胜. 2016. 口译的心理认知与记忆策略. 江苏外语教学研究，（4）: 3.

2 Clark, J. & Paivio, A. 1991. Dual coding theory and education. *Educational Psychology Review*, 3(3): 149–210.

少需记忆的信息单位数量，减轻短时记忆的负荷[1]。在听到一段话时，先理解大意，将零散的内容理顺并归纳串联为几大要点，会更便于记忆。

练习 3

请听录音，录音结束后请用源语复述。

2.4 记忆训练方法

2.4.1 复述

复述法是信息逻辑化、视觉化和组块化训练的有效策略。此方法要求译员听取完整段源语信息后，不借助笔记进行内容复述。在初级阶段，建议以简短、结构逻辑明晰、贴近口语的材料为基础，用源语复述，目标为确保内容结构完整、逻辑明确。随着练习的深入，应增加材料长度和复杂度，如选择逻辑不甚连贯的内容，并转向目的语复述。在保证结构和逻辑明晰的基础上，逐渐强化对细节的回忆。

2.4.2 影子跟读

我们在第 1 单元提及了影子练习或称影子跟读，这个训练方法可以很好地锻炼听力、反应能力和注意力，这些能力对记忆的效果也有很大影响。练习时，译员需用同一种语言跟读发言人的讲话，练习材料应难度从简到繁，语速从缓到快。随着能力的提升，可以尝试以下三个阶段的进阶：

阶段 1：源语跟读与复述

保持一个合理的听译时间差，在最初阶段几乎可以和源语同步开始，尽量跟上源语的语速，将讲话内容完整准确地跟读出来。经过一段时间的训练后，可逐渐增加内容难度，在源语开始半句话到一句话时再开始跟读源语。跟读结束后，可再用源语进行内容复述。

---

[1] 庄鸿山，肖晓燕. 2004. 英语口译资格证书考试培训教程. 厦门：鹭江出版社.

阶段 2：注意力分配干扰练习

跟读的同时在纸上写数字，比如从 1 到 100、从 100 到 1，锻炼多任务处理（multi-tasking）的能力。

阶段 3：目的语复述与跟读

针对同一篇文本，第一遍练习用源语跟读发言，第二遍紧跟着发言人用目的语复述或概括，这一遍已经相当于同声传译了，难度较大。大家也可以尝试在源语跟读后，边听录音边看着原文进行目的语复述，相当于视译，这部分将在第六单元进一步学习。

2.4.3 储备常用知识

如果一段话的词句涉及记忆中的相关知识点或经验，就更容易对信息进行理解、组织并串联成更大的组块来记忆。这要求口译员在平时训练中不仅要记单词，也要多积累和记忆不同主题的常用短语、习语、句型句式等的中英表达。比如，从一个商务议题、术语或专有名词引申到一个相关短语、句子、故事等更大的组块，积累不同领域的背景知识，从而形成长期记忆。这样口译员就能在听到相关发言时，凭借长期记忆快速反应和处理信息，减轻短期记忆负荷，尤其是针对不同商务场合的一些套话、开场词、感谢词、结束语、祝福语的常见句型和内容，应多加归纳总结和储备。

以下是商务对话场合的一些通用表达：

如何称呼您？How do I address you?

您看什么时间比较方便？What time would be convenient for you?

希望您通融一下。We hope that you could accommodate us.

洽谈中请你们多加关照。I'd appreciate your kind consideration in the coming negotiation.

希望能与您达成生意/交易。I hope to conclude some business with you.

我们期待能与贵公司合作。We are looking forward to cooperating with your company.

祝您生意兴隆。I wish you success in your business transaction. / Wish you a prosperous business.

我还不能马上说定。I can't say for certain off-hand.

成交！Let's call it a deal.

2.5 口译练习

练习1

Text 1

请听录音。这是 Cyrus Janssen 在 TEDx 上的演讲，讲述了自己在中国生活长达十年后学到的道理。请先预习词汇，在听录音过程中尝试使用本单元学到的记忆策略，进行源语复述和影子跟读练习。录音已分割为多个语段，进行复述练习时请在提示音（beep）后暂停录音并开始复述，进行影子跟读练习时无须暂停录音且不可阅读原文。建议多次练习，不断进阶练习难度。

词汇预习

佛罗里达州立大学	Florida State University
城市人口流动	urban migration
爱荷华州	Iowa
两极分化的	polarized

Text 2

请听录音。本文改编自阿里巴巴创始人马云在德国汉诺威消费电子、信息及通信博览会开幕式上的主旨演讲。请先预习词汇，在听录音过程中尝试使用本单元学到的记忆策略，进行源语复述、目的语复述和影子跟读练习。录音已分割为多个语段，进行复述练习时请在提示音（beep）后暂停录音并开始复述。

词汇预习

汉诺威	Hannover
主流	mainstream
数字经济	digital economy
敏捷性	nimbleness

练习2

Dialogue 1

四人小组对话口译练习两人为讲者，两人为译员。当然，你也可以扫码进行自主练习，在提示音（beep）后进行口译。

词汇预习

生产潜力	potential for production capacity
代理人	agent
佣金	commission
发票	invoice
繁荣的，成功的	prosperous
小册子	booklets
目录	catalogues
代理合同	agency agreement

Dialogue 2

四人小组对话口译练习，互换讲者和译员角色。同样，你也可以进行自主练习。

词汇预习

谈判代表	negotiator
报价	quotation/offer
性价比高	cost-effective
名称，绰号	moniker

Dialogue 3

四人小组对话口译练习，自选讲者和译员角色。同样，你也可以进行自主练习。

词汇预习

高端电子产品	high-end electronic products
智能穿戴设备	smart wearables
保密	confidentiality
知识产权	intellectual property rights
工艺流程	process

2.6 练习原文、译文及解析

练习1

原文：

面对全球化的市场挑战，我们需要不断调整和优化我们的企业战略。随着科技的迅猛发展，我们必须紧跟时代的步伐，采用新的数字化解决方案来提升我们的竞争力。在这个过程中，我们要牢记客户的需求，以客户为中心，为他们提供定制化的解决方案。

然而，市场的不确定性也给我们带来了挑战。一些不可预见的因素可能会影响我们的业务运营，这就需要我们保持灵活性，随时做出调整。同时，我们也要关注可持续发展，积极推动绿色环保理念，为我们的业务创造更长久的价值。

在未来的道路上，我们需要保持创新精神，不断探索新的商机。我们要加强团队协作，激发每个成员的潜力。虽然前方的路途充满了挑战，但我们坚信，在我们的努力下，一定能够取得更大的成功。

练习解析：

这段发言逻辑相对清晰，内容一是面对全球化市场要做些什么，其中谈到了数字化方案和定制化；二是面对不确定的市场要做些什么，包括保持灵活性和可持续发展；三是展望未来。在听原文的过程中，尝试在脑海中画脑图（mindmap），将逻辑信息捋顺。请再次听录音，看看能否抓住逻辑，通过脑图或其他形式辅助记忆。

练习 2

原文：

I'd like to talk to you today about why men hate shopping.

If there's one thing that clearly shows that men and women are different, it's shopping. Women like to window shop and browse whereas men shop with a mission. Men know exactly what they want to buy before they leave the house. Women, however, tend to decide on their purchases only after they've seen what's available in stores.

Men easily get lost in shopping malls. Women spend so much time there. They can give shortcuts to the security staff.

Women don't get stressed if a short shopping trip turns into a very long shopping trip. Men, on the other hand, insist on being in and out of the store in twenty minutes, otherwise they will suffer from sudden increases in their blood pressure.

(Adapted from a video from Speech Repository— "Why Men Hate Shopping")

练习解析：

你的脑海中是否有这样几幅画面：一边是极具目的性、非常清楚自己要购买什么的男性，一边是慢悠悠逛街的女性；一边是在大商场里迷了路的男性，一边是对商场了如指掌，甚至知道商场里捷径的女性；一边是逛街超过20分钟就血压飙升的男性，一边是逛了很久仍兴致勃勃的女性。

如果在脑海中情景再现，是否复述起来就更简单了呢？请再听一遍，看看信息视觉化是否能够帮助记忆。

练习3

原文：

Artificial intelligence is reshaping industries across the globe. Its applications range from healthcare and finance to manufacturing and entertainment. AI's ability to analyze vast amounts of data and make predictions is dramatically changing decision-making processes. However, concerns about data privacy and ethical considerations must also be addressed. Governments and organizations are collaborating to establish regulations and guidelines for the responsible AI implementation. As AI continues to evolve, its impact on society and the workforce cannot be underestimated.

练习解析：

尝试将段落信息变成信息块串联起来，可以想象一下在脑海中有一排抽屉，整合大块的信息点作为抽屉的标签，每个抽屉中依次填入对应的短小信息单位（图2-1）。当然，随着抽屉里的信息逐渐增多，记忆可能无法承载，我们可以依靠笔记法来分担一部分的记忆压力。不过在这个阶段，你可以努力将信息进行分析组块，争取将大块信息点记录下来。

图2-1　信息组块化

练习 4

Text 1

原文：

Two weeks prior to my graduation from Florida State University, the Dean looked at me and said, "Cyrus, what are your plans after graduation?" And I dropped a bomb on everybody when I said I bought a one-way ticket to Shanghai. I'm moving to China, I decided to start my professional career in China. Now originally I went to China on a one-year work contract and that 1 year contract ended up being ten. //

Now when you start working in China, you'll quickly realize that the Chinese people are actually some of the hardest working people that you'll ever meet. There's a phrase that has been trending in Chinese internet over the last two years and that is 996. What this refers to is working from 9:00 in the morning till 9:00 in the evening, six days a week. //

Now, this 72-hour work week and nearly double what we are used to here in the west, just gives an insight and a testament to why the Chinese economy is growing so fast and rapidly these past few decades. //

The Chinese work incredibly hard. They work 51 straight weeks out of the year and they get one single holiday per year, seven days off during Chinese New Year or Spring Festival as we call it in China. //

And being in China during Spring Festival truly is an absolutely amazing event, because it is the largest urban migration in the entire world. You have hundreds of millions of people crowding into buses, into trains, planes, automobiles, whatever they can, and traveling twenty, thirty, sometimes 40 hours to make it home so they can spend China's most important holiday with their family. //

That is the first lesson—no matter what you achieve in life, whether it is financial success, career success, or maybe international fame, nothing is more important than your family. //

Now, this principle I applied directly to my life. You know, as an American expat that was living in China, I went home once a year back to Florida, my hometown. But along the way, I would make it a point to go to a very small town in Iowa to visit my grandmother. This was really one of the most rewarding experiences of my life, because my grandmother and I didn't see each other a lot when I was living in America. //

But all of a sudden, when I lived in China, it now became an annual visit. Ironically, out of all of her grandchildren, I was the only one that made an annual visit to Iowa to see her. And ironically, I was living 7,000 miles away on the other side of the world. But no matter what you do in this life, never forget your family. //

Another important lesson that I ever learned in China came during my very first year in China. Now we became at the end of a very long work week. Like I mentioned, we had a 6-day work week, and at the end of the 6-day work week, three young Chinese colleagues came up to me and they said, "Cyrus, will you join us tonight for dinner?" //

And they would go down to the market. They would buy a big fish, some pieces of meat, some vegetables, and a case of beer. And they would cook an amazing meal using a single element stove and a single frying pan. And we sat down. //

They said, "Cyrus, we're so excited that you would come and eat with us. You know we're so excited about being here in Shanghai. All of us left a small village. We all came here to get a better job, to have a better life." I really thought to myself. I'm not much different than these three young men. I, too, also came to Shanghai, because of a job opportunity, I also want better things in my life. I also want to work hard and achieve success. //

Sure, we look different, we have different skin colors, we have different language, different religion. But at the end of the day, we're more similar than we are different. And this is a really important point that I think everybody needs to realize. //

Now working in China truly is one of the most amazing experiences and it's important to really understand the culture and to really form these relationships. It's important to start learning Chinese. And learning Chinese is one of the most amazing endeavors that I've ever gone on in my life. I've been learning Chinese for 14 years now, and it is something that I will continuously learn. // Now I would encourage everybody to go out and learn a foreign language. It doesn't have to be Chinese. There can be any language in the world. Because by learning a foreign language, you're going to start cultivating your mind. You're gonna have a challenge that is going to give you confidence to tackle many other things in this world. //

But my motivation for learning a language really came from a quote from Nelson Mandela. When he said, when you speak to a man in a language that he understands, it goes to his head. But "when you speak to a man in his mother tongue, it goes to his heart." //

You see, we live in a world that is very polarized and very divided. Unfortunately, many people today form their opinions by looking at headlines and reading social media posts. Now, it's really important to remember that you don't change the world with your opinion, you change it with your actions. So go out there and be the change that you want to see in the world today. Thank you. //

(Adapted from Cyrus Janssen's speech at TEDx)

练习解析：

对话口译中，译员通常面对的是口语化甚至即兴的讲话。此篇为贴近日常工作和生活、较为口语化的演讲，且涉及中国特色知识。针对此类讲话，可调动长期记忆，利用已有的知识储备帮助理解和记住大意，理顺逻辑，将看似零散的内容简化归纳为更大的组块来记忆。同时，将讲者所述的故事在脑海中联想转换成具体的画面场景，以加深记忆。

信息组块化： 全篇围绕讲者在中国工作生活的经历及从中学到的道理，可归纳为三大组块：一是发现中国人工作非常努力，但非常重视春节，讲者通过春节认识到家人的重要性，因此每年都会看望祖母；二是通过与中国同事相处、与同事一起吃晚餐的经历，思考自己与之的异同，认识到大家都是为了美好生活而努力，彼此之间更多的是相似之处而非差异；三是通过学习中文的体验，引申到鼓励学习外语和用行动改变世界。

信息逻辑化：本篇第1段中涉及多个短句，句子之间没有逻辑连词，且过去时和现在时混用，需要根据涉及的时间点和时态找到语句间的逻辑关系，即"一是回顾毕业前两周：买了单程票去上海，打算搬到中国，因为我决定在中国工作；二是谈现在的状态：起初我签的是1年的工作合同，结果一待便是10年"。

信息视觉化：本篇第10段衔接上文描述了同事请吃晚餐的日常生活场景，可利用信息视觉化的策略，将源语提到的食物和用具以图像的形式呈现在脑海，想象"同事去市场买鱼肉菜酒后，用一个灶台一口锅做一顿丰盛的菜，然后我们坐下一起吃晚餐，同事对我的加入表示欣喜"这一场景，便于记忆和表述。

Text 2

原文：

女士们，先生们，大家晚上好。

记得14年前，我第一次来到汉诺威，租了一个小摊位，尝试在欧洲卖中国制造的产品。我花了很长时间找摊位，那时汉诺威还没那么繁荣，但那次展销会很成功。摊位不好找，我们最后拿下了一个小摊位，但很少有人注意到我们。

八年前，我们再次来到这里，想让所有小摊位挂到阿里巴巴上进行在线销售，但是失败了，因为那时的人们还不能理解网购。

今天我再次来到这里，目的是寻找目前互联网产业丢失的一环。过去20年互联网产业取得巨大成功。不过，有一件事情很奇怪，我发现很少有互联网公司能健康、平稳地活过三年。换句话说，互联网公司可能只有蜜日、蜜周，但蜜月就不一定有了。为什么会这样？问题出在哪里？缺失了什么？//

如果一个行业内很多公司活不到三年，那么这个行业就不可能成为主流行业，不可能实现数字经济。因此，我们想知道该如何找到解决问题的办法。

未来，制造商会自己研制机器，这些机器不仅可以生产，还会说话，会思考。机器不再依靠石油、电力，但是依靠数据。

未来，企业不再关注规模，标准化和力量，而会关注灵活性、敏捷性、个性化和用户友好性。

我也坚信，未来还会出现更多的女性领导者，因为人们关注的不仅是力量，还有智慧、善良和责任。//

我们处于最好的时代，创造力、奇思妙想爆发的时代，我们每个人都在努力实现梦想。不论什么行业，不论是货车司机、游戏玩家，或所有的资深人士，每个人都可以充分利用科技实现梦想，这在以前是不可想象的。有了数据，所有梦想都实现了。

我相信，不是科技改变了世界，是科技背后的梦想。如果是科技改变了世界，我不会出现在这里，因为我不是个技术控，对计算机一无所知，对互联网也只是略知一二。但是，我有一个强大的梦想，就是帮助中小企业。//

所以，14年前我带着中国商品来到这里，但没有成功。14年后，我们要通过互联网帮助欧洲的中小企业开拓中国市场，乃至世界市场。是梦想在改变世界，而不是技术本身。

所以，女士们，先生们，让我们努力工作吧。这是一个精彩纷呈的世界，这是一个属于年轻人的世界，这是一个属于未来的世界。

非常感谢大家的倾听。//

（改编自2015年3月15日德国汉诺威消费电子、信息及通信博览会开幕式上阿里巴巴创始人马云的主旨演讲）

参考译文：

Ladies and gentlemen, good evening!

I remember 14 years ago, when I first came to Hannover, I tried to rent a small booth to sell the Chinese products to Europe. It took us a long time to look for the booth, and at that time Hannover was not that prosperous, but the fair was very successful. It was difficult to get a booth. Finally, we got a small booth, but very few people noticed us.

Eight years ago, we came back again. We tried to help all of the booths move online and sell on Alibaba. It did not work because at that time people didn't understand what online shopping was.

Today I come back again to find the important missing part of the Internet industry. The Internet has been pretty successful in the past 20 years. But one thing I find very strange is that very few Internet companies can survive peacefully and healthily for more than three years. That means most of the Internet companies can only have honey days, honey weeks but maybe not honey months. What is the problem, and what is the missing part? //

If many companies in an industry cannot survive for three years, that industry can never become mainstream and can never achieve a digital economy. So what we want to do is to find a solution to this problem.

In the future, all the manufacturers will make machines that can not only produce products, but also talk and think. The machines will no longer rely on oil or electricity, but on data.

Business will not focus on the size, standardization and power. They will focus on the flexibility, nimbleness, customization and user-friendliness.

Also, I strongly believe that in the future world, we are going to have a lot of female leaders because people not only focus on the physical strength, but also wisdom, kindness, and responsibility. //

We are at a great time of innovation, inspiration, invention and creativity, and I think everyone is working hard to realize their dreams. Truck drivers, game players, and all those professionals in different industries can leverage technology to realize their dreams, which is unimaginable in the past. Everything becomes possible with data.

And I strongly believe that it's not the technology that changed the world, but rather the dreams behind the technology. If the technology alone changed the world, I wouldn't be here because I'm not a tech guy, and know nothing about computer, and know very little about the Internet. However, I have a strong dream to help small and medium-sized enterprises. //

14 years ago, I came here to sell Chinese products but failed. 14 years later, we are helping the European small and medium-sized businesses to explore the Chinese market and even the world market by using the Internet. It's the dreams that drive the world, not the technology.

Ladies and gentlemen, let's work hard. It's a fantastic world. It's the globe that belongs to young people. It's the world that belongs to the future.

Thank you very much for listening. //

练习解析：

本文讲述了讲者在过去的 14 年中不断尝试进入欧洲市场的经历，可以通过信息逻辑化、信息视觉化和信息组块化协助记忆和理解。

信息逻辑化：在录音的第一个语段，讲者提到了他在汉诺威的三次经历，分别是 14 年前、8 年前和 2015 年的当天。这三个时间点是文本的逻辑结构，可以帮助记忆和理解该语段。

信息视觉化：想象一下讲者在第一次来到汉诺威时寻找小摊位的场景，然后想象他再次来到汉诺威，试图将小摊位挂到阿里巴巴上进行在线销售的情景。这种视觉化的想象有助于记忆和理解故事中的关键事件。

信息组块化：将文本分成几个关键部分，如讲者的过去经历、互联网产业的问题和挑战等。每个部分都可以作为一个信息组块，有助于记忆和组织思路。

通过这些记忆策略，我们可以更轻松地理解和记忆整段演讲，从而更好地传达演讲的内容和情感。

练习 5

Dialogue 1

原文:

A: Hello. Mr. Li. I am glad to meet you here at the trade fair.

B: 我也很高兴。请坐。您有什么需要的吗?

A: Thank you. It seems that your business is prosperous. There are many customers here.

B: 是的,还可以吧。销量每年都在提高,而且我们的生产潜力还很大。

A: What do you think about appointing a commission representative or agent overseas to boost your sales?

B: 这个主意不错。不过,目前我们在国外已有几位代理人了。请问您的代理区域是哪里?

A: We are interested in becoming your agent for machine parts in Australia. What do you think?

B: 不错,我们正好也想开拓澳洲市场。

A: So, what is the typical commission rate for your agents?

B: 佣金的话一般是 4%。

A: But 4% is too low. You see, we have a lot of work to do in sales promotion, such as advertising on radio or TV, printing booklets, catalogues and so on. 4% cannot cover all costs.

B: 别担心,如果你们的销量能超出我们的预期,我们会提高佣金的比例。

A: So? You are saying...

B: 我们希望可以在澳洲售出 500 万美元的货物,如果你们的销量超过这个数的话，我们可以考虑将佣金提高到6%。

A: Good. How do you pay the commission?

B: 我们可以直接从发票金额中扣除佣金，或在付款后汇给你方。

A: All right. If it's okay, we would like to sign an agency agreement with you immediately.

B: 希望您考虑一下，我们也很期待能与贵公司合作。

A: Thanks for your support.

参考译文：

A: 您好，李先生，很高兴在交易会上见到您。

B: Likewise. Please have a seat. What are you interested in?

A: 好，谢谢。看起来您生意很兴旺，这么多客户光临。

B: Yes. Not bad. Our sales are booming year after year. And we still have great potential for production capacity.

A: 哦，你们是否想在国外选择一家代理商或代理人为你们推销产品？

B: That's a good idea. However, we have several agents overseas. Where is your agency located?

A: 我们可以在澳洲做您方的机器零件代理人，不知你们意下如何？

B: That's great. We also want to explore the Australian market.

A: 那么，你们通常给代理人的佣金率是多少？

B: We typically offer a 4% commission to our agents.

A: 但是4%太低了。你知道，为了推销产品，我们要做很多工作。比如，在电台或电视上做广告，印刷小册子、商品目录等。这一切花销，4%是不够的。

B: Don't worry. If your sales volume exceeds our expectations, we will increase the rate.

A: 您的意思是……？

B: We hope to sell goods worth 5 million dollars in Australia. If your sales exceed this figure, we can consider increasing the rate to 6%.

A: 不错。那么，佣金如何支付？

B: We may either deduct the commission directly from the invoice value or remit it to you after payment.

A: 那好。如果可以，我们会与你们立即签订代理协议。

B: Please think it over. We are also looking forward to collaborating with your company.

A: 感谢您的支持。

练习解析：

原文均为短句，只要理解讲者逻辑和掌握商务英语常用词，记忆和翻译都不难。其中"We have a lot of work to do in sales promotion, such as advertising on radio or TV, printing booklets, catalogues and so on. 4% cannot cover all costs."此句列举了多个推销手段，可归纳为"广告印刷"这一个组块来记忆，从而把主要精力放在记忆句子逻辑要点，即推销工作多，花销不止4%的佣金。翻译时再结合自己的常识来回忆"广告印刷"的细节，即常见的电台或电视广告、手册目录印刷等。

Dialogue 2

原文：

A: A warm welcome to the negotiators from the Chinese "Eat Well" Food Company. Welcome to Italy! I am Vivi, the general manager of MACHI Chocolate Production. This is my business card.

B: 很高兴见到你，Vivi 女士，我是中国"吃得好"食品公司的采购经理 Aria。这是我的名片。我们对贵公司的巧克力很感兴趣。

A: We are honored that you are interested in our company's products. Do you have any requirements?

B: 我们公司打算在今年八月份之前订购 5 000 盒贵公司的巧克力。

A: Here is a price list of our products. Our offer is $100 per box for orders of less than 10,000 boxes.

B: 我知道贵公司产品的性价比很高。但是这个价格超出我方接受范围。请问能否提供 30% 的折扣呢？

A: Our chocolate is acclaimed internationally for its taste, often surpassing many renowned brands. It has earned the moniker "chocolate gold" both domestically and globally. We never offer discounts.

B: 我们了解贵公司的巧克力质量优越。但你们的要价实在太高了，我方无法接受。

A: We have fully considered this price. Of course. If you are able to increase the purchase volume to more than 10,000 boxes, the quotation can be reduced to $90 per box.

B: 10 000 盒已经远远超过了我方的需求。听说你们已经生产了大量的巧克力，如果不尽快寻找销售渠道，你们所承担的成本和风险将会更大。相信我方庞大的销售网络和成熟的营销技能必定能够给予你们帮助。

A: Thank you for being considerate for us. We also hope that your company can bring larger markets for our products. As a token of sincerity, we are willing to reduce the original price to $92 per box.

B: 我方接受 92 美元一盒的报价。这是我们拟订好的合同。如果没有异议，请在下方签上您的名字。

A: Okay, I'm glad we could come to an agreement. I look forward to our collaboration.

参考译文:

A: 欢迎来自中国"吃得好"食品公司的谈判代表来到意大利，我是MACHI巧克力生产公司的总经理Vivi。这是我的名片。

B: Nice to meet you, Ms. Vivi. I am Aria, the purchasing manager of China's "Eat Well" Food Company. Here is my business card. We are interested in your chocolate.

A: 很荣幸您对我们公司的产品感兴趣，您有什么要求呢？

B: Our company intends to order 5,000 boxes of your chocolate by August this year.

A: 这是我们产品的价格表，订购量在10 000盒以下，我方的报价是100美元一盒。

B: I understand that your products are very cost-effective, but the price is still unacceptable. Could you give us a 30% discount?

A: 您知道国际上我们公司的巧克力口感优于多家知名巧克力生产公司，且以"巧克力黄金"的美誉享誉海内外。我方从来不提供折扣。

B: We understand that your chocolate is of superior quality. But your price is too high for us to accept.

A: 我方是经过充分的考虑才报出这个价的，当然如果你们可以把采购量提升到10 000盒以上，报价可以降低至90美元一盒。

B: 10,000 boxes are far beyond our requirements. We heard that you have produced a large amount of chocolate. If you do not find a sales channel as soon as possible, you will bear higher costs and risks. We believe that our extensive sales network and well-developed marketing skills will certainly help you.

A: 谢谢贵方能为我方考虑。我方也希望通过贵公司将我方产品推向更大的市场。为表诚意，我方愿意将原报价降至 92 美元一盒。

B: We accept the offer of $92 per box. This is the contract we have worked out. If there are no objections, please sign your name at the bottom.

A: 好的，很高兴能达成此次协议，希望我们合作愉快。

练习解析：

原文涉及两家公司的中英文名称和公司情况，以及 "As a token of sincerity 为表诚意" 这样的通用表达。在真实的口译场合下，应做好译前准备，储备公司基本背景知识和一些通用表达，可减轻记忆负担。此外，针对 "10 000 盒已经远远超过了我方的需求。听说你们已经生产了大量的巧克力，如果不尽快寻找销售渠道，你们所承担的成本和风险将会更大。相信我方庞大的销售网络和成熟的营销技能必定能够给予你们帮助。" 此类中长句，先理清信息的逻辑层次会更便于记忆，即我方不需要那么多盒——你方的大量巧克力如不尽快销售则成本和风险增加——而我方可协助你方销售。

Dialogue 3

原文：

A: 你好，我是 A 公司的代表，很高兴能够与贵公司进行商务洽谈。

B: Hello, I am a representative from Company B, and we are also delighted to collaborate with a high-tech company like yours in China. Do you have any specific ideas or directions in mind for our cooperation?

A: 我们希望能够与贵公司共同研发和生产高品质的电子产品，并在全球市场进行销售。我们可以提供技术和强大的产能支持，同时也希望能够得到贵公司关于技术上的合作和支持。

B: This sounds very promising, and we are also looking forward to collaborating with your company. Could you please specify the types of products you are specifically interested in cooperating on?

A: 我们希望能够合作生产智能手机、平板电脑等高端电子产品，以及智能穿戴设备等其他产品。

B: These are all products with significant market potential. Do you have any specific suggestions for our cooperation plan?

A: 我们可以共同研发生产产品，并通过营销策略卖到全球市场。我们可以互派员工进行合作交流。我们也可以提供适合中国的市场调研结果，帮助你们推行本土化策略。

B: These are excellent collaboration suggestions. Regarding the cooperation agreement, do you have any specific requirements or terms you would like to discuss?

A: 我们希望能够达成互惠互利的合作协议，并明确双方的权利和义务。同时，我们也希望能够达成合理的价格和合适的付款方式，以便更好地保障双方的利益。

B: These are very reasonable requests, and we also hope to reach a mutually beneficial cooperation agreement.

A: 对了，我们还希望能够在协议中明确保密条款和知识产权方面的问题，以及在产品质量和售后服务等方面达成共识。

B: These are indeed crucial issues, and we take confidentiality and intellectual property matters seriously. We can sign confidentiality and intellectual property agreements together and enhance management and supervision throughout our cooperation. Moreover, we will rigorously maintain product quality and ensure customer satisfaction through our after-sales service.

A: 非常感谢，我们也会为贵公司提供最好的合作支持和服务。请问在合作过程中，你们需要什么帮助吗？

B: We may require some guidance in technique and process, and your assistance in marketing and sales will also be valuable. We hope that we can learn and grow together through our collaboration.

A: 非常感谢你们的信任和支持，我们会尽我们最大的努力为贵公司提供优质的合作服务和支持。希望我们的合作能够取得更加圆满的成果。

B: Thank you very much for your efforts and support. We also hope to achieve a win-win outcome together. Looking forward to a successful collaboration with better outcomes.

参考译文：

A: Hello, representing Company A, I am pleased to engage in business negotiations with your company.

B: 你好，我是B公司的代表，我们也非常高兴能与你们这样的中国高科技公司合作。请问你们在合作上有什么具体想法或倾向吗？

A: We are interested in collaborating with your company to jointly develop and manufacture high-quality electronic products for the global market sales. We can offer technical expertise and robust production capabilities. Additionally, we are seeking your company's technical cooperation and support in this endeavor.

B: 这听起来非常有前景。我们很期待与你们公司合作。请问你们具体希望合作的产品类型是什么？

A: We are interested in collaborating to manufacture high-end electronic products, such as smartphones, tablets and other devices like smart wearables.

B: 这些都是有巨大市场潜力的产品。请问在合作方案上，你们有什么具体的建议吗？

A: We can collaborate on joint research and product development, as well as implement marketing strategies to access global markets. We can exchange employees for collaborative work. Additionally, we can provide market research tailored for China to assist you in implementing localization strategies.

B: 这些都是非常好的合作建议。请问在合作协议方面，你们有什么具体的要求或想商议的条款吗？

A: We aim to establish a mutually beneficial cooperation agreement that outlines the rights and responsibilities of both parties. Additionally, we would like to negotiate fair pricing and suitable payment terms to better protect the interests of both sides.

B: 这些都是非常合理的要求，我们也希望能够达成互惠互利的合作协议。

A: Well, we also intend to include confidentiality clauses and address concerns regarding intellectual property in the agreement. It's also important to establish a consensus on product quality and after-sales service within the agreement.

B: 这些都是非常重要的问题，我们也非常重视保密和知识产权的问题。我们可以共同签署保密协议和知识产权协议，并在合作过程中加强管理和监督。同时，我们也会严格把关产品质量，在售后服务上确保客户满意度。

A: Thank you very much. We will also provide the best possible support and service to your company. Is there anything we can help with during our collaboration?

B: 我们可能需要一些技术和工艺流程方面的指导，在市场营销和销售方面也可能需要你们的协助。希望我们可以在合作过程中互相学习和进步。

A: Thank you very much for your trust and support. We will do our utmost to provide your company with high-quality cooperation, service and support. We hope that our collaboration will achieve even greater success in the future.

B: 非常感谢你们的付出和支持，我们也希望能够共同实现双赢局面。期待我们合作顺利，取得更好的成果。

练习解析：

　　原文对话整体逻辑清晰，有一些寒暄的通用表达，比较容易记忆和翻译大意。其中也存在少部分信息较多的段落，包含多个并列句和并列词。在无笔记口译时，需在理解整段内容大意基础上留意信息之间的逻辑关系和关键词，理清并列的主要信息后，再将并列的关键词串联起来。通过组块化记忆，减少需记忆的信息单位。比如："我们可以共同研发生产产品，并通过营销策略卖到全球市场。我们可以互派员工进行合作交流。我们也可以提供适合中国的市场调研结果，帮助你们推行本土化策略。"这一段有三个并列的合作计划，可先提炼需重点记忆并翻译的动词，即"研产销、互派、调研本土化"，自然可联想到其对象分别是"产品、员工和市场"，然后通过对原话的整体理解来回忆并串联起其余内容即可。

第 3 单元

口译笔记法

口译笔记法是口译员学习的基本技能，常用于交替传译。Seleskovitch[1]曾指出，用笔记辅助可以增强注意力，有助于口译员及时回顾和记忆信息。此外，笔记有助于放松大脑记忆，因为短期记忆无法做到牢记讲者的每一个细节。笔记将帮助口译员回顾讲者表达的主要想法，使用符号语言进行逻辑连接，有条理地传达讲者的中心思想。

3.1 口译笔记的特征

口译笔记不同于速记，具有以下四大特征[2]：

3.1.1 即时性

口译笔记仅用于帮助译员在短时间内立即记住发言内容，并用目的语传达。口译结束后，笔记无须再使用或给他人查看，因此记录关键信息即可，不宜过度依赖笔记。

3.1.2 简约性

发言人的语速通常比逐字记录的速度快，因此口译员需要用最简约易懂的关键字和符号来记录发言内容，而非记录完整词句。

3.1.3 逻辑性

做笔记时，译员应首先理解源语，理顺逻辑，并通过记录文字及符号组合准确反映发言内容的逻辑关系。

3.1.4 个性化

口译笔记只为译员自己服务，因此可按个人的习惯和偏好记录，也可创造符号，形成个人符号系统。

---

1 Seleskovitch, D. 2002. Language and memory: A study of note-taking in consecutive interpreting. In F. Pöchhacker & M. Shlesinger (Eds.), *The Interpreting Studies Reader*. London: Routledge, 121–129.

2 邹丽. 2014. 浅谈口译笔记的特点和原则方法. 校园英语，(21): 179.

3.2 口译笔记的内容

Rozan[1]曾提到笔记主要是提醒口译员一眼就能看到需要翻译的语段、讲者的想法及各语段之间的联系；同时，笔记也是为了便于口译员进行流畅而地道的翻译。Phelan[2]也认为，口译员应该避免为了记下讲者所说的一切内容，而忽略对发言内容、其主题或论点的分析，后者才是记笔记过程中的关键。事实上，笔记只是帮助口译员去回忆演讲内容和结构的整体框架。

口译笔记从内容上可分为文字笔记和非文字笔记。文字笔记包括短语、单字、汉字部首、缩写词、字母、阿拉伯数字、罗马数字等，非文字笔记可包括标点符号、数学符号、图形、箭头、线条等。译员可根据书写效率自主选择用源语或目的语记录，以确保尽可能快速记录，跟上讲者语速。

记笔记并不意味着把听到的每一个单词都记下来，口译员应该把关注点放在发言内容的中心思想上，因为译员手写的速度无法和讲者说话的速度实现同步。除了中心思想，记下各个意群、语段之间的联系也很重要，因为它们决定了发言内容的整体意义。口译员解读笔记时需要特别注意表示后果、原因和效果的连词和从属词等。有时，记住专有名词、数字、术语等在口译过程中比较困难。因此，口译员需要做好充分的译前准备，并结合语境进行翻译。最后，要注意动词时态、条件从句和句子的结构等，因为它们能影响句子的整体意思。

3.3 口译笔记的方法

3.3.1 笔记符号

如何有效地记笔记是学习笔记过程的关键环节。鉴于跟随讲者的语速进行笔

---

1 Rozan, J. F., Gillies, A. & Waliczek, B. 2004. *Note-taking in Consecutive Interpreting*. Poland: Tertium.

2 Phelan, M. 2001. *The Interpreter's Resource*. Sydney: Multilingual Matters Ltd.

记极具挑战性，笔记应该秉承高效原则，使用缩写和符号来节省时间。初学者可以参考前辈的笔记符号，经过反复练习，创建自己的笔记符号体系。总体而言，笔记符号因人而异，但需要时刻牢记笔记的作用是辅助翻译，不应本末倒置，为了记笔记而忽视听力训练和对发言内容的理解。下面是常见的口译符号。

1. 数学符号

∵（因为，由于，幸亏）: because, due to, thanks to

∴（所以，因此，结果是）: so, therefore, consequently

=（相同，一致，公平）: the same as, equal to, similar to

>（大于，超过，高于）: surpass, exceed, more than, superior to

<（少于，低于）: less than, inferior to

+（另外，多）: plus, add, moreover, besides

–（减去，除去，除了）: minus, deduct, except

2. 惯用符号

:（看，说，想，评论）: speak, express, think

!（危险，警告，当心，值得注意的）: dangerous, warning, alarming, alert, hazardous, perilous, jeopardy, watch out, sure, certainly, of course

__（这个，强调）: underline, emphasize

e.g.（例如，比如）: for example, such as

3. 图形符号

□（国家，民族）: nation, state, republic, kingdom, federal, union

☆（重点，重心，重视；重要的，主要的，杰出的）: important, significant, key, crucial, critical, meaningful, essential, outstanding, distinguished, marked, remarkable, notable, excellent, perfect, eminent; wonderful, terrific, fantastic, fabulous, marvelous, chief, primary, main, major, dominant; emphasize, stress, focus, underscore, highlight, attach great importance to, pay attention to

$（美元，钱；有钱的，富裕的）: dollar, money, rich, well-off

U（协议，决议，合约，条约）: agreement, treaty, contract, covenant, compact, convention, resolution

æ（行动，行为，法案）: action, act

4. 趋向符号

↓（影响，效果，压力，负担）: influence, effect, affect, impact, have bearing on, pressure, stress, burden, load

←（邀请，需要，访问，来到）: be invited, needed, come (here)

→（去，到，走）: to, go (there)

↑（增加，提升，提高，升级，升值）: increase, improve, enhance, grow, advance, rise, raise, promote, go up

↓（减少，下降，降低，贬值）: decline, decrease, reduce, drop, fall, devalue, degrade, cut down, go down, fall off

5. 英文字母

y（年）: year

m（月）: month

w（周）: week

h（小时）: hour

m（分钟）: minute

d（日子，今天）: day, today

t（明天）: tomorrow

- 2y（两年以前）: two years ago

b（但是）: but, however, nevertheless

c（世纪）: century

e（经济）: economy, economics

f（金融）: finance, financial, financially

句子精练

听录音，做口译笔记并进行口译。请注意，本单元末的译文及笔记仅供参考，并不要求与其完全一致。

3.3.2 笔记布局

口译笔记一般使用专门的笔记本，其宗旨是方便译员在记录和翻译过程中翻页查看。口译本每页中间有一条红色的竖线，一般记录完左侧再记录右侧。整本正面记录完毕之后，再反面记录，而不是一页正反两面都写完再用下一页。在长交传中，译员往往需要记录多页笔记，纵向翻页和单面记录方便译员在讲者结束一段发言后快速翻回该段发言笔记的开始点。

口译笔记布局一般遵循以下三大原则[1]：

1. 纵向记录

口译笔记宜纵向延伸，以便清晰体现原文结构和逻辑关系，使译员能迅速浏览笔记和输出译文。其中，记录主语、谓语、宾语时，可采用对角线方向书写，将其分成三行，分别安排在笔记的左、中、右部分。这样能快速帮助译员识别句中的各种成分，方便读取。

2. 少字多划

除了字词以外，译员可以灵活应用各种符号、箭头、线条等符号来代替冗长的源信息，使笔记更为简练，用尽量少的笔记表达尽量多的信息。

---

[1] 邹丽. 2014. 浅谈口译笔记的特点和原则方法. 校园英语,（21）: 179.

3. 明确结束

口译中，讲者的上一段话和下一段话之间，必须有明确的界限。上一次的结束点即下一次翻译的开始点，一般用双斜线等符号表示。

3.4 口译练习

练习 1

Text 1

请听录音，这是施耐德电气首席执行官 Jean-Pascal Tricoire（赵国华）在中国发展高层论坛举办前的演讲。请先预习词汇，在听录音过程中尝试记笔记，并进行交替传译。录音已分割为多个语段，请在提示音后暂停录音并开始口译。

词汇预习

施耐德电气	Schneider Electric
中国发展高层论坛	China Development Forum (CDF)
释放潜力	tap into the potential
研发和制造	R&D and manufacturing
价值链	value chain
全方位复苏和强大韧性	all-round recovery and resiliency
志同道合的伙伴们	like-minded people

Text 2

请听录音，本文节选自习近平主席于 2022 年 6 月 22 日在金砖国家工商论坛开幕式上的主旨演讲。请先预习词汇，在听录音过程中尝试记笔记，并进行交替传译。录音已分割为多个语段，请在提示音后暂停录音并开始口译。

词汇预习

金砖国家工商论坛	BRICS Business Forum
步履维艰	to face strong headwinds
市场化、法治化、国际化营商环境	market-oriented, law-based, and internationalized business environment
投资兴业	invest and do business

练习 2

Dialogue 1

四人小组对话口译练习,两人为讲者,两人为译员。当然,你也可以通过扫码进行自主练习,在提示音后进行口译。

词汇预习

深圳旅游文化大会	Shenzhen Tourism and Culture Conference
平安国际金融中心	Ping An International Finance Center
京基 100	KingKey 100 Tower
"湾区之光"摩天轮	Bay Glory Ferris Wheel
欢乐港湾	OH Bay
锦绣中华中国民俗文化村	Splendid China (China Folk Culture Villages)

Dialogue 2

四人小组对话口译练习,可互换讲者和译员角色。同样,你也可以进行自主练习。

词汇预习

漫天要价	intend to be exorbitant
批发价	wholesale price
最高价格	price ceiling
签到台	registration desk

Dialogue 3

四人小组对话口译练习,自选讲者和译员角色。同样,你也可以进行自主练习。

词汇预习

百威啤酒有限公司	Budweiser Co., Ltd.
首次采购	initial purchase
有竞争力的报价	competitive quotation
续约	extend partnership / renew or extend the contract
美国山姆会员商店	Sam's Club
可购性,(价格)承受力	affordability

3.5 练习原文、译文及解析

本节的口译笔记示范(图 3-1~图 3-17)仅供参考,练习时无须完全一致。

句子精练

1. **原文**:由于今年人力成本提升,我们的报价比去年高。

参考译文：Because the labour cost has increased this year, our quoted price will be higher than last year.

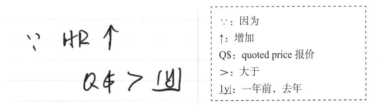

图 3-1　参考笔记及讲解（1）

2. **原文**：我想强调的是，交货时间对我们很重要。

参考译文：I want to emphasize that the delivery time is very important to us.

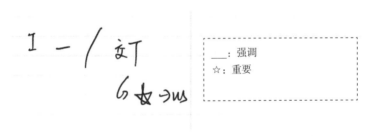

图 3-2　参考笔记及讲解（2）

3. **原文**：According to our agreement, our commission fee is 3%.

参考译文：根据协议内容，我们的佣金为3%。

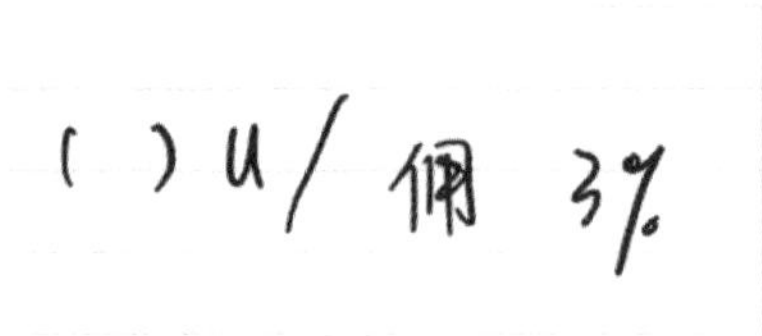

( )U/ 佣 3%

( )：根据
U：协议

图 3-3　参考笔记及讲解（3）

4. **原文**：全年国内生产总值增长 3%，居民消费价格上涨 2%。

   参考译文：The Gross Domestic Product (GDP) of the year grew by 3%. The Consumer Price Index (CPI) rose by 2%.

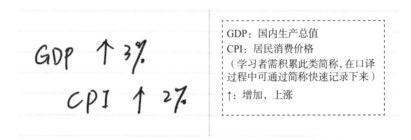

GDP：国内生产总值
CPI：居民消费价格
（学习者需积累此类简称，在口译过程中可通过简称快速记录下来）
↑：增加，上涨

图 3-4　参考笔记及讲解（4）

5. **原文**：Although countries around the world have taken countermeasures, the Covid-19 pandemic has still made enormous impact on the global economy.

   参考译文：尽管各国采取了各种应对措施，然而新冠疫情仍然对全球经济造成了巨大的冲击。

Al：although，虽然，尽管
□s：国家，s 为复数结尾
//：但是
↓：影响
◯'：global，全球的
eco：economy，经济

图 3-5　参考笔记及讲解（5）

笔记符号因人而异，口译学习者应在练习中总结积累自己的常用符号。同时，在已知特定主题的情况下，应尽可能积累相关词汇储备，并提前想好相关符号。

练习 1

Text 1

原文:

Hello! I'm Jean-Pascal Tricoire, the Chairman and CEO of Schneider Electric. I'm really so happy to be back with the community of the China Development Forum in person, soon in Beijing.

The key words today for China's modernization are high-quality development and opening-up at a higher level. //

Starting with high-quality development, this requires more innovation and more collaboration. China is already well known for its high-level innovation. We've seen gigantic progress in Artificial Intelligence, big data, software and other cutting-edge technologies. This has empowered the upgrade and transformation of industries. //

A Chinese Modernization will certainly come with opening-up at a higher level. International collaboration is critical to both R&D and manufacturing. We admire China's progress over the past years on its openness. With this evolution, we believe that the potential of both domestic and international markets will be tapped into further and innovation of the country can be unleashed to a greater extent. //

Schneider Electric entered China 35 years ago. Thanks to the opening-up policy, we've been continuously expanding our footprint. Today the Chinese market has become our second largest market in the world and is one of the four global hubs covering the whole value chain from R&D, upstream purchasing, production, sales into services. //

With the opening up at even higher standard, foreign partners could play a more important role in meeting the increasing demand of the huge domestic market and being a bridge to the international market. With this, we remain confident in China being a critical driver for the 2023 world economy with its all-round recovery and its resiliency. //

Finally, I expect that CDF 2023 is convening at a very relevant time, where like-minded people can come together after three years' virtual communication to discuss and debate over many important issues regarding China and the world. //

Nothing compares to face-to-face interaction. I am thrilled to participate, and look forward to feeling the pulse here, and to gaining some deep insights on how we international companies can contribute more to the journey forward. //

参考译文：

大家好！我是施耐德电气董事长兼首席执行官赵国华。很快就能在北京和中国发展高层论坛的伙伴们见面，我感到非常高兴！

我认为，今日中国现代化的关键词是"高质量发展"和"更高水平的对外开放"。//

首先是高质量发展，这需要更多的创新与合作。中国凭借高水平创新闻名于世，在人工智能、大数据、软件和其他尖端科技领域的进展也广受瞩目。这些都推动了产业的升级和转型。//

中国的现代化必将伴随着更高水平的对外开放。国际合作对于研发和制造都至关重要。我们钦佩近年来中国在扩大开放上取得的成果。由此我们相信，这一进程将会进一步释放国内和国际市场的潜力，更大程度地激发创新。//

得益于对外开放的政策，施耐德电气植根中国35年以来，不断加大投资。今天，中国已经是我们全球第二大市场以及涵盖全价值链（从研发、采购、生产、销售到服务）的四大中心之一。//

伴随着更高标准的对外开放，外资企业可以更好地发挥价值，满足快速增长的国内巨大市场需求并成为中国衔接国际市场的桥梁。我们相信中国的全方位复苏和强大韧性将为2023年的世界经济注入关键推动力。//

2023年的中国发展高层论坛恰逢其时，经过三年的线上交流，我期待和志同道合的伙伴们相聚，讨论有关中国和世界的诸多重要议题。//

没有什么能比得上面对面的交流，我很高兴能参与其中，并期待亲身感受这个国家的脉动，深入了解跨国公司如何为中国的现代化进程做出更多贡献。//

参考笔记：

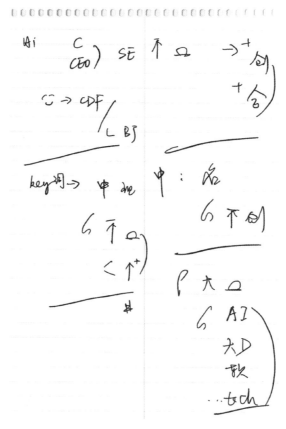

图3-6　参考笔记及讲解（6）

注释：

└: future

<: open up

#: 结束标记

C/CEO/SE/CDF/BJ/AI 等：英文缩写

⌒: development

+: more

): 并列项

↻: 逻辑连接符

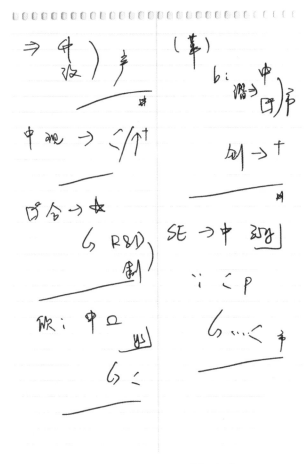

图 3-7　参考笔记及讲解（7）

注释：

📱：international

b：believe

☆：critical

∵：因为

⌋：ago

…：continuously

（革）：通过 / 经过改革

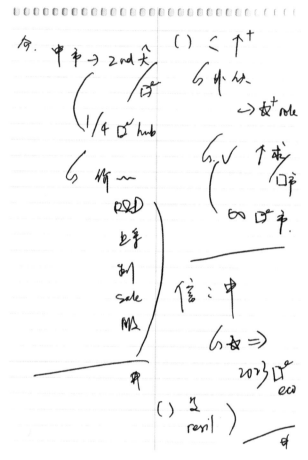

图 3-8　参考笔记及讲解（8）

注释：

大̂：最大（ˆ最）

□：国内，国内的

价﹏﹏：价值链

∞：连接，桥梁

☆⁺：more important

⇒：推动

∨↑求：满足增长的需求

resil：resilience

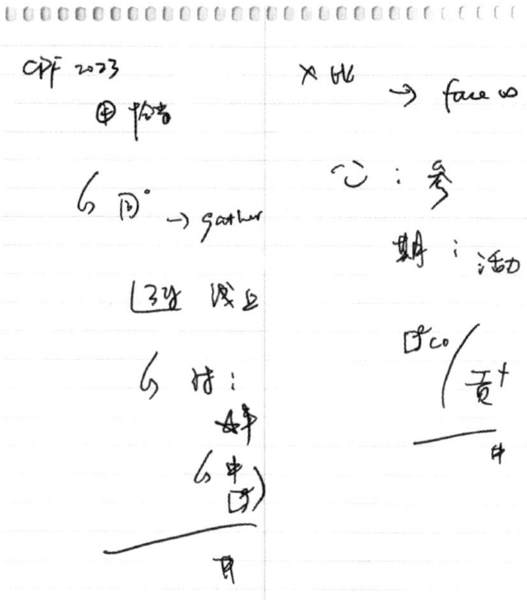

图3-9 参考笔记及讲解（9）

注释：
⊕: convene，召开
同°：志同道合的人，°表示"人"
face ∞: face-to-face interaction
co: companies

Text 2

原文：

尊敬的各位同事，

各位工商界朋友，

女士们，先生们，朋友们：

很高兴出席金砖国家工商论坛。首先，我向各位嘉宾表示诚挚的欢迎！//

当前，世界百年变局和世纪疫情相互交织，各种安全挑战层出不穷，世界经济复苏步履维艰，全球发展遭遇严重挫折。// 世界向何处去？和平还是战争？发

展还是衰退？开放还是封闭？合作还是对抗？是摆在我们面前的时代之问。//

　　历史长河时而风平浪静，时而波涛汹涌，但总会奔涌向前。尽管国际形势风云变幻，但开放发展的历史大势不会变，携手合作、共迎挑战的愿望也不会变。// 中国将继续提高对外开放水平，建设更高水平开放型经济新体制，持续打造市场化、法治化、国际化营商环境。热忱欢迎大家在中国投资兴业，加强经贸合作，共享发展机遇。//

（节选自2022年6月22日习近平主席在金砖国家工商论坛开幕式上的主旨演讲。）

参考译文：

Dear Colleagues,

Members of the Business Community,

Ladies and Gentlemen,

Friends,

　　I am glad to attend the BRICS Business Forum and wish to extend a warm welcome to all of you. //

　　Right now, our world is facing drastic changes and a pandemic both unseen in a century. Various security challenges keep emerging. The world economy still faces strong headwinds on its path toward recovery, and global development has suffered major setbacks. // Where is the world headed: Peace or war? Progress or regression? Openness or isolation? Cooperation or confrontation? These are choices of the times that we are confronted with. //

　　Human history, like a river, keeps surging forward, with moments of both calm waters and turbulent waves. Despite changes in an evolving global environment, the historical trend of openness and development will not reverse, and our shared desire to meet challenges together through cooperation will remain as strong as ever. // China will continue to pursue opening-up against higher standards, develop new systems for a higher-standard open economy, and continue to foster a market-oriented, law-based, and internationalized business environment. I warmly welcome you to invest and do business in China, strengthen business cooperation with China, and share in China's development opportunities. //

参考笔记：

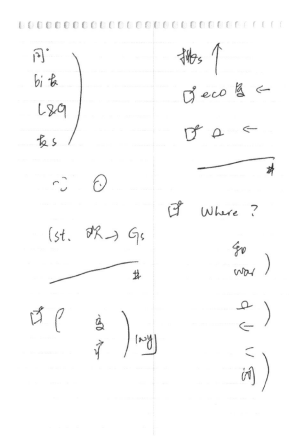

图 3-10　参考笔记及讲解（10）

注释：

bi: business

友 s / Gs：朋友们 / 各位嘉宾，s 表复数

☉：会议，论坛

疒：疾病，疫情

↑：增多

←：艰难，遇到挫折；衰退

ρ：看见，面对

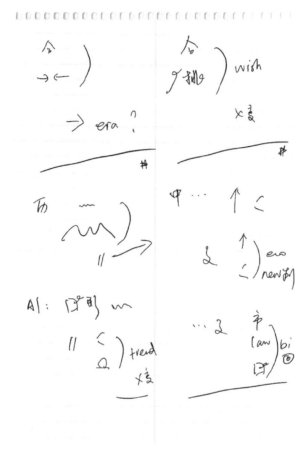

图 3-11　参考笔记及讲解（11）

注释：

→←：对抗

﹏﹏：风平浪静

~~~：波涛汹涌

Al：although

//：but

ρ：应对

廴：建设
◎：环境

图 3-12 参考笔记及讲解（12）

注释：

Inv: invest　　　　　　　　　　　　　+：加强

练习 2

Dialogue 1

原文：

A: 第一届深圳旅游文化大会如期召开，欢迎各位记者朋友的到来。请这位记者开始提问。

B: Could you provide a brief overview of the current state of Shenzhen's tourism industry?

A: 随着全球旅游业快速发展，旅游规模快速扩大，深圳作为一线城市，每天都接待游客超 15 万人次。

B: As far as I know, landmark buildings are iconic areas of the city that foreign tourists must visit. May I ask what the landmark buildings in Shenzhen are?

A: 深圳是一个高速发展的城市，你很难想象 40 年前这里还是个小渔村，如今有平安国际金融中心、京基 100、"湾区之光"摩天轮等地标性建筑。平安国际金融中心于 2016 年竣工，总高度达到 599.1 米，共 118 层。游客可在 116 层观景台远眺全城景观。"湾区之光"摩天轮则位于欢乐港湾内，是深圳上空最高的摩天轮，总高 128 米。你可以在傍晚坐上摩天轮，尽情欣赏浪漫的晚霞和湾区风光！

B: It's well known that Shenzhen's bustling commercial areas are major tourist attractions, significantly boosting its tourism industry. However, the industry's growth can't depend solely on these commercial hubs. What other standout tourism assets does Shenzhen offer?

A: 深圳是一个开放包容的城市，不是只有大商场。我想给你介绍我们的锦绣中华中国民俗文化村，你可以在此体验中华民族的风土人情和传统习俗，更加深刻地了解中华文化。

B: The government plays an important role in the development of the tourism industry. May I ask what measures the Shenzhen Municipal Government has implemented in 2022 to promote the development of the tourism industry?

A: 在 2022 年，我市发放各类帮扶旅游企业资金超 1.16 亿元，惠及市场主体 1 200 家。今年我市出台六项阶段性措施，以推动恢复文体旅游市场活力。

B: Thank you very much for answering the questions.

参考译文：

A: The 1st Shenzhen Tourism and Culture Conference convened as scheduled. I would like to welcome the friends from the press. I will now take questions from this reporter.

B: 您能简要介绍一下深圳市旅游业的发展状况吗？

A: With the rapid development of the global tourism industry and the rapid expansion of tourism market, Shenzhen, as a first-tier city, receives more than 150,000 tourists every day.

B: 据我所知，地标性建筑是城市的代表性区域，是外来游客的必游之地。请问深圳市的地标性建筑有哪些？

A: Shenzhen is a rapidly developing city. It's hard to believe that just 40 years ago, it was a small fishing village. Today, it boasts landmarks like the Ping An International Finance Center, KingKey 100 Tower, and the Bay Glory Ferris Wheel, among others. The Ping An IFC, a 118-story skyscraper finished in 2016, soars to 599.1 meters. From its 116th-floor observation deck, visitors can witness panoramic views of the city. Located at the OH Bay, the Bay Glory Ferris Wheel is Shenzhen's tallest, standing at 128 meters. You can ride the ferris wheel at sunset and view the romantic evening glow and the stunning view of the bay area.

B: 众所周知，深圳市繁荣的商业区是主要旅游景点，为深圳的旅游业发展提供了强劲的动力。但旅游业的发展不能只靠繁荣的商业区，请问您认为深圳市还有哪些出色的旅游资源？

A: Shenzhen is an open and inclusive city, and we have more than just big shopping malls. I would like to introduce that we have Splendid China (China Folk Culture Villages), where you can immerse yourself in the local and traditional customs of the Chinese nation, gaining a deeper understanding of Chinese culture.

B: 政府在旅游业的发展中发挥着重要作用。请问2022年深圳市政府为促进旅游业的发展采取了哪些措施？

A: In 2022, the city distributed more than 116 million yuan of funds to support tourism enterprises, benefiting 1,200 market entities. This year, Shenzhen has adopted six temporary measures to boost the vitality of the culture, sports and tourism market.

B: 非常感谢您的回答。

参考笔记：

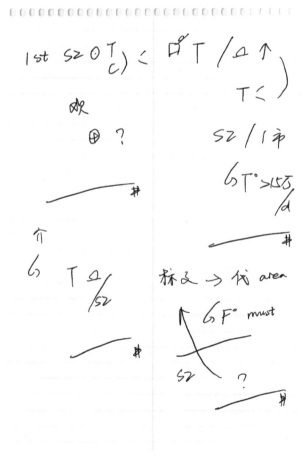

图 3-13　参考笔记及讲解（13）

注释：

T: tourism，本文笔记固定 T 含义　　　　/d：每天

〈：召开，扩张等　　　　　　　　　　　廴：建筑

T°/F°: tourists, foreigners　　　　　　　↰：指示符号，指引至前面记录过的内容

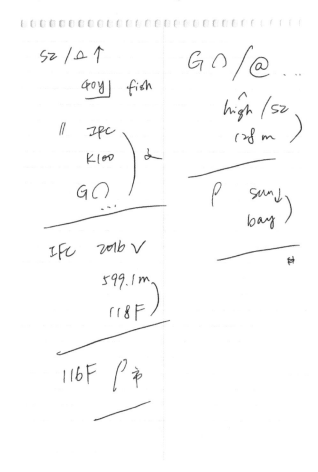

图 3-14　参考笔记及讲解（14）

注释：

⌒：视觉化即时符号，摩天轮

m/F: 英文缩写，meter, floor

√：完成，竣工
@：at

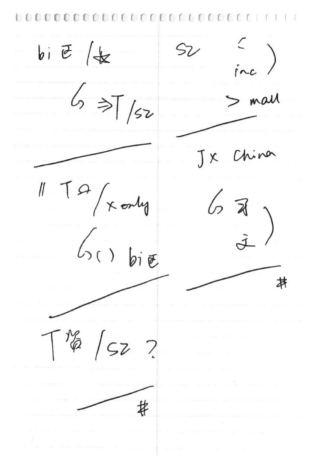

图 3-15　参考笔记及讲解（15）

注释：

inc: inclusive

JX China: 锦绣中华

＞：more than，不止

资、习、文：资源、习俗、文化（用一字代替一词）

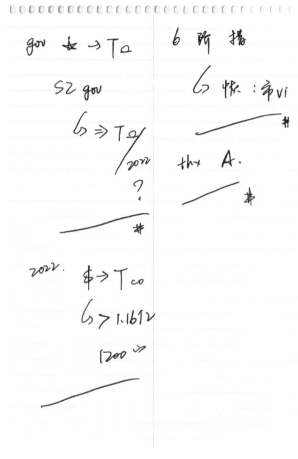

图 3-16 参考笔记及讲解（16）

注释：

gov: government

宀：家

$: 资金

vi: vitality

练习解析：

1. **原文**：第一届深圳旅游文化大会如期召开，欢迎各位记者朋友们的到来。请这位记者开始提问。

参考译文：The 1st Shenzhen Tourism and Culture Conference convened as scheduled. I would like to welcome the friends from the press. I will now take questions from this reporter.

解析：口译笔记符号包括不同类型，如英文缩写类："深圳"为 SZ（其他地名同理，可在练习中不断积累），"平安国际金融中心"为 IFC；特殊符号类：⊙ 表示"会议"，〈表示"召开"，⊕ 表示"开始"；使用英文单词首字母或中文词汇单字甚至部首表示整个词汇，如 T 代表 tourism，C 代表 culture，"欢"表示"欢迎"等。面对记者招待会等重要场合时可以提前进行译前准备，积累相关词汇，也可在词汇预习部分提前想好对应的笔记符号。

2. **原文**：As far as I know, landmark buildings are iconic areas of the city that foreign tourists must visit. May I ask what the landmark buildings in Shenzhen are?

参考译文：据我所知，地标性建筑是城市的代表性区域，是外来游客的必游之地。请问深圳市的地标性建筑有哪些？

解析：口译笔记的布局一般随着手部书写的挪动，从左到右、从上至下，换行后会往右缩进，呈纵向对角线书写。句子中或句子与句子间的逻辑关系可使用符号→等进行标注。

图 3-17　参考笔记及讲解（17）

Dialogue 2

原文:

A: 欢迎光临深圳"明华堂"汉服时装展览会。我是本次展览会的负责人,您叫我小陈就行。

B: Hello, I am Smith from the United Kingdom. From the registration desk, I see that this year's event has attracted more attendees from UK. It's really getting more exciting, and I owe it all to you.

A: 哪里哪里,史密斯先生您太夸奖了。不知道您今天来到我们展会有没有别的什么想法?

B: My primary purpose for this visit is to learn about Chinese culture and purchase a few Hanfu outfits to bring back to England. If your prices are suitable, we would be interested in placing an order immediately.

A: 我们的定价大约是一套 100 美元左右。您也知道近几年劳动力和原材料成本增加了很多。我们的报价是以成本和合理的利润为依据,不是漫天要价。

B: I understand, but it is indeed a bit expensive! Is it possible to lower the price further, let's say $50 per outfits? Also, I don't require you to cover the shipping costs for me.

A: 史密斯先生,确实不太能再降低价格了,我们卖给您的价格已经是批发价了,如果再降低价格的话,我们便没有利润可言了。

B: However, if that's the case, I am afraid there is no need for us to continue the discussion. I feel so sorry that we will have to cancel the entire transaction. Can't we meet each other half-way and find a mutually beneficial price for both of us?

A: 我的意思是我们不可能把价格降到你方提出的标准,差距太大了。考虑到我们的产品质量,您会发现我们的价格是很有竞争力的。

B: Well, if it's $20, I'll take it immediately and get three more.

A: 好的，感谢您的参观，由于这个最高价格是我的领导定的，我得先和他请示一下。

B: That's alright. I hope we can finalize the deal. I look forward to hearing from you soon.

参考译文：

A: Welcome to the "Minghua Tang" Hanfu Fashion Exhibition here in Shenzhen. I am the person in charge of this exhibition, you can call me Chan.

B: 您好，我是来自英国的史密斯。我在签到台发现今年的展览会吸引了更多的英国参会人员，这个活动真是越办越精彩，我觉得都是你的功劳。

A: Oh, Mr. Smith, you flatter me. May I ask what is the main purpose of your visit today?

B: 我来到这个展会的首要目的是了解中国文化，顺便购买几套汉服带回英国。如果你们的价格合适，我们可以马上定购。

A: Our pricing is approximately around $100 per outfit. As you may be aware, labor and raw material costs have increased significantly in recent years. Our pricing is based on cost considerations and a reasonable profit margin, and it is not intended to be exorbitant.

B: 我理解，但是确实有点贵啊！能不能再便宜一些，50美元一件如何？你看我也不需要您为我垫付邮费。

A: Actually, Mr. Smith, the price we're offering is already at the wholesale rate. We can't reduce it further without losing our profit margin.

B: 但是如果那样的话，恐怕我们也没有必要再谈下去了。很遗憾，我们不得不取消整个交易。难道我们就不能互相妥协各退一步，找到一个对双方都有利的价格吗？

A: What I mean is that it's not possible for us to lower the prices to what you've suggested; the price gap is large. Considering the quality of our products, you will find that our prices are very competitive.

B: 这样子吧，降价 20 美元，我立刻购买并且多购买三件。

A: Ok, thanks for visiting, I don't think I have the authority to break that price ceiling set by my superior. I think I have to report to him for further decision.

B: 好的，希望我们能达成交易，期待您的回复。

练习解析：

在现实情况下，针对此类对话的口译通常属于商务陪同口译，并不需要做笔记，此类较简短的对话可以选择无笔记交传练习。

本篇有比较口语的表达，如"哪里哪里，史密斯先生您太夸奖了"。千万不能照字面译为"Where where"，也不必纠结"太夸奖"要如何照字翻译，英文中有类似的表达"You flatter me"。

遇到不太懂的表达也要注意联系上下文，以帮助理解。例如"Can't we meet each other half-way and find a mutually beneficial price for both of us?"，如果听到"meet each other half-way"不理解是什么意思的时候，不可放弃后边的听力，结合"find a mutually beneficial price for both of us"可以理解该句应为"互相妥协各退一步""找到一个对双方都有利的价格"。

Dialogue 3

原文：

A: My name is Alex, the purchasing manager of Sam's Club in America. First, I would like to extend my warm welcome to your arrival.

B: 您好，我是百威啤酒有限公司的谈判代表，您可以称呼我为吴女士。十分感谢您的热情招待。

A: Welcome. We are greatly looking forward to collaborating with your company, and it is truly our privilege. Nowadays, customers shopping at our supermarket have shown a gradual increase in their demand for beer, making our supermarket an excellent choice.

B: 是的，我公司之前已经对您方做了一个初步的了解，知道你们在啤酒这方面有非常良好的市场，所以我们非常开心能在今天就我们双方的合作事宜进行洽谈。

A: It's evident that Budweiser excels in packaging, flavor and affordability. For our initial purchase, we are interested in acquiring one hundred thousand cases. Can you give us a competitive quote for that amount?

B: 非常感谢您对我们百威啤酒的认可，鉴于我们是初次合作，我公司可以给到您每箱五十美元的价格，您看是否可以呢？

A: Considering the substantial size of this order, I would like to inquire whether it's possible for you to offer a more competitive price.

B: 是这样的，因为我们的啤酒在国内外都有较高的知名度和受到市场认可，所以结合我们的品质我认为这个报价是很合理的，或者您方觉得什么价格比较合适呢？

A: I would prefer if the price per case of beer could be lowered to $30. After all, I hope that our collaboration can have a positive start, which would be conducive to maintaining our friendly relationship.

B: 其实我们也有对近来美国的啤酒市场作详细调查，我们了解到的市场平均价格是高于您方所提价格的两倍，所以我们认为贵方的这个报价不太合理。

A: You should know that we are the largest chain of supermarkets in the United States, with a highly stable and extensive customer base. If we can establish a long-term partnership, it has the potential to generate greater profits for your company in the future.

B: 好吧，对于未来的销售额我们暂且不谈，毕竟未来的发展都是未知的嘛。但由于我公司是真诚希望我们双方能达成合作的，所以如果您方同意在售卖时将我们的啤酒摆放在超市货架的前端的话，我们可以接受这个价格。

A: Certainly, we will place Budweiser beer at the front of the supermarket shelves. Thank you for accepting our quotation. We look forward to establishing a long-lasting partnership with your company.

B: 当然可以，如果合作默契的话，我方也会考虑进一步续约。

参考译文：

A: 您好，我是 Alex，美国山姆会员商店的采购部经理。首先，我想对您的到来表示热烈的欢迎。

B: Hello, I am the negotiator of Budweiser Co., Ltd. You can call me Ms. Wu. Thank you so much for your hospitality.

A: 欢迎您吴女士。我们非常期待与贵公司的合作，这是我们的荣幸。现如今在我们超市消费的客户对啤酒的需求逐渐增加，因此我们的超市是一个非常好的选择。

B: Yes. Previously, we conducted some preliminary research about your company and are aware of your strong presence in the beer market. Therefore, today we are very pleased to discuss about the potential cooperation between our two companies.

A: 显然，百威在包装、口味和价格方面都表现出色。对于我们的首次采购，我们有兴趣购买十万箱。您能否为这个数量为我们提供一个有竞争力的报价？

B: Thank you very much for your recognition of our Budweiser beer. Since this is our first collaboration, we can offer you a price of $50 per case. Would that work for you?

A: 鉴于我们这笔订单非常大，我想知道您是否能给我到一个更具有竞争力的价格呢？

B: Understood. Given the high level of recognition and market acceptance of our beer both domestically and internationally, I believe the offered price is quite reasonable, considering our product quality. If you have a specific price range or any preferences in mind, please feel free to share, and we can explore the possibilities together.

A: 我更希望每箱啤酒的价格能够下调至 30 美元。毕竟我希望我们的合作能有一个好的开始，便于维持我们友好的关系。

B: Actually, we have conducted a thorough investigation into the recent beer market in the United States. Our findings show the average market price is nearly double your proposed rate. Therefore, we find your proposed quotation to be somewhat unreasonable.

A: 您要知道我们是美国最大的连锁超市，有非常稳定和广泛的客户群体。如果能建立未来长久的发展，这可以为贵公司提供更多的利润。

B: Well, let's not dwell on future sales figures, as the future is indeed uncertain. However, since we genuinely wish to establish a partnership between our two companies, if you agree to have our beer prominently displayed at the front of the supermarket shelves, we can accept the price you've proposed.

A: 当然可以，我们会将百威啤酒放在超市货架的最前端。感谢您接受我们的报价。我们希望与贵公司建立长久的合作关系。

B: Certainly, if our partnership thrives, we're open to extending it in the future.

练习解析：

在实际商务谈判场合中，译员一定要提前知晓谈判双方、谈判方向等相关内容，并做好译前准备，例如，山姆会员商店和百威啤酒有限公司可以简写为 SC/Sam 和 BW/bud，可快速记录。谈判中每段发言通常不长，译员主要通过脑记来进行翻译，可以只记录关键词，比如数字来辅助记忆。

UNIT 4
第 4 单元

数字口译

在商务谈判、经贸会议、文化旅游等商务情境中常常会出现数字。在汉英、英汉口译中，数字翻译常令初学者乃至资深译员感到困扰。由于中英在数字的分段及表述上存在差异，这增加了翻译过程中的出错风险。一方面，纯粹依赖记忆数字较为困难，译员通常需采用笔记以辅助记录；另一方面，译员必须迅速将所记数字转译为目标语言。因此，本单元将专注于数字的口译技巧及其双语转译。

4.1 英汉数字表达差异

4.1.1 英文数字表达

在英语中，计数习惯每隔三位为一个段位，从第二段位（即千位）开始，以千（thousand）、百万（million）、十亿（billion）为分隔，因此，对照阿拉伯数字读数时相对简单，只要确认最高位属于哪一段位即可顺利读出。请遮住表4-1右栏，尝试用英文读出左栏数字。

表 4-1 英文读数

阿拉伯数字	英文读法
789,123	Seven hundred and eighty-nine thousand, one hundred and twenty-three
4,567,890	Four million, five hundred and sixty-seven thousand, eight hundred and ninety
2,345,601	Two million, three hundred and forty-five thousand, six hundred and one
6,789	Six thousand, seven hundred and eighty-nine
987,123	Nine hundred and eighty-seven thousand, one hundred and twenty-three

4.1.2 中文数字表达

在汉语中，基数词的每一个位次都有固定的单位，如十、百、千、万、十万、百万、千万、亿、十亿、百亿、千亿、万亿等汉语数字在读数时是以阿拉伯数字四位为一段。请遮住表4-2右栏，尝试用中文读出左栏数字。

表 4-2 中文读数

阿拉伯数字	中文读法
1,234,567,890	十二亿三千四百五十六万七千八百九十
987,654,321	九亿八千七百六十五万四千三百二十一
123,456	十二万三千四百五十六
1,000,000,000,000	一万亿
567,890	五十六万七千八百九十

由于汉语数字并不像阿拉伯数字的书写一样以三位为一段，因此在读数的时候需要进行一定的转换。我们可以从低位数开始，每四位为一段位画线辅助，如 12/3456/7890，9/8765/4321。当然，这并不是最快的方法。由于阿拉伯数字与英文数字的读数分段一致，我们可以在看到阿拉伯数字时用英文思维去理解这个数字是多少，然后再转换为中文。这个过程在后文双语转换中会进一步阐述，也可以通过表 4-3 对比英汉数字表达的差异。

表 4-3 英汉数字表达差异

1	,	0	0	0	,	0	0	0	,	0	0	0	,	0	0	0
万亿		千亿	百亿	十亿		亿	千万	百万		十万	万	千		百		
t				b				m				th				

练习 1

请分别用英文和中文读出下列数字：

7,892,301	543,210,987
25,678,912	1,234,567,890
135,789,456	987,654,321
9,871,543	56,789,123
67,890,123	6,543,210

4.2 数字的笔记及双语转换

在口译过程中,译员听到数字后要如何记录在笔记本中?是写中文、英文还是阿拉伯数字?这并没有固定的要求,可以根据自己的习惯,同时也要考虑目的语是中文还是英文。如果在听和记的过程当中有精力,可以进一步进行信息加工,将数字用目的语记录下来,这样在产出环节会更加顺畅。

四位数(千位)及以下:

因为不涉及段位转换,建议直接用阿拉伯数字记录,不管是用中文还是英文都可以快速读出。

五位数(万位)及以上:

从"万"开始,英汉数字的记录则可考虑多种方式相结合,如阿拉伯数字、汉字、小数点和英文单词缩写等。

练习 2

听录音,做笔记记下每一个数字,并分别用中英文读出。

听完录音,你是否发现,源语为中文或英文时,记录方式有所不同?你是否习惯用源语进行记录,是否发现有时无法记录下来,或者是记下来后转换出现困难?请翻至 P82-83 查看针对数字的笔记以及讲解。当然,记录和转换的方法因人而异,上述笔记仅供参考,希望你在练习过程中能找到适合自己的笔记方式和转换技巧。

4.3 倍数的翻译

倍数的翻译常常会出错,但是只要记住中英文中针对倍数分别各有两种常用表达方式,即可顺利译出。

中文：

A 是 B 的 x 倍。

A 比 B 大 / 小（形容词）x-1 倍。

英文：

A is x times as large/small (*adj.*) as B.

A is x times larger/smaller (comparative *adj.*) than B.

以上四个句子表达的都是同一个意思。如果仍然有些困惑的话，我们一起看一下以下的句子。

英文：

This year's turnover is twice as large as that of last year.

This year's turnover is twice larger than that of last year.

中文：

今年的销售额是去年的两倍。

今年的销售额比去年增长了一倍。

发现了吗？英文中不管是哪种表达，倍数的数字不变；但中文则在"大 / 小……倍"的表达中要减去 1。

其他倍数表达：

1. "to increase/decrease by a factor/multiple of x (to increase/decrease by x times)"：表示以 x 倍增加 / 减少，即增加 / 减少了 x 倍。
2. "to increase/grow/decrease xfold"：x 仍为数字，如"threefold""fivefold"等，表示增加 / 减少了几倍。此表达可以没有对比项。

练习 3

请阅读以下句子并进行视译练习，即阅读的同时即刻进行口译。

1. The new manufacturing process is five times more efficient than the previous method.
2. The company's revenue increased by a factor of three after the successful product launch.

3. The company's market share has grown sevenfold in the past two years.
4. 新的软件系统比旧系统快二十倍。
5. 由于出现意外挑战，项目的完成时间比预计多了两倍。
6. 公司的利润相较于去年增加了三倍。

口译练习

数字口译练习

听录音，做笔记记下每一个数字，并依次译出。

句子练习

请听录音并做笔记，在提示音后进行口译。请注意对数字的记录，同时不要忽视数字对应表达的含义。

练习 1

Text 1

请先预习词汇，听录音，并进行带笔记交传。本文节选自美国商务部副部长 Don Graves 在波多黎各经济对话上的演讲，录音已分割为多个语段，请在提示音后暂停录音并开始口译。请注意对数字的记录，同时不要忽视数字对应表达的含义。

词汇预习

美国商务部	the U.S. Department of Commerce
波多黎各（位于西印度群岛东部的岛屿）	Puerto Rico
群岛	archipelago
美国救援计划	American Rescue Plan

| 美国国家海洋和大气管理局 | The National Oceanic and Atmospheric Administration (NOAA) |

Text 2

请听录音,本文节选自国务院总理李强在 2023 年 3 月 5 日第十四届全国人民代表大会第一次会议上所作的政府工作报告,涉及过去一年国家在商务、经贸领域的工作。请先预习词汇,在听录音过程中尝试记笔记,并进行交替传译。录音已分割为多个语段,请在提示音后暂停录音并开始口译。

词汇预习

港口集疏运效率	loading, unloading and transport efficiency in ports
稳岗扩就业	stabilize and increase employment
营商环境	business environment
市场主体登记管理	market entity registration and administration
个体工商户	individually owned businesses / self-employed individuals
中小企业	small and medium-sized enterprises (SMEs)
实物商品	physical goods
零售额	retail sales
跨境电商综试区	integrated pilot zones for cross-border e-commerce
海外仓	overseas warehouses
外商投资法	the Foreign Investment Law
外商投资环境	the business environment for foreign investors
"一带一路"沿线国家	Belt and Road Initiative (BRI) countries
对外投资	outbound investment
健康有序发展	sound and orderly development
境外风险防控	overseas risk prevention and control

练习2

Dialogue 1

四人小组对话口译练习，两人为讲者，两人为译员。当然，你也可以通过扫码进行自主练习，在提示音后进行口译。

词汇预习

国内的	domestic
新西兰田园牛奶供应公司	New Zealand Pastoral Milk Supply Company
周转时间	turnaround times
加速，推进	expedite
订单高峰期	peak order seasons
手头未交货的订单	back orders
填补库存	replenish inventory
优先安排发货	give priority to one's order concerning delivery

Dialogue 2

四人小组对话口译练习，可互换讲者和译员角色。同样，你也可以进行自主练习。

词汇预习

国际名酒展览会	International Wine Exhibition
展位，展台	booth, stand
酒商代表	wine merchant representative
玛姆（某一酒品牌）	Mumm
光地展位	bare booth / bare space

Dialogue 3

四人小组对话口译练习,自选讲者和译员角色。同样,你也可以进行自主练习。

词汇预习

生产线	production line
不良率	defect rate
信用度	creditworthiness
中国银行纽约分行	Bank of China's New York Branch
商会	chamber of commerce

4.5 练习原文、译文及解析

数字中英文表达	参考笔记	解析
Two thousand, three hundred and six 两千三百零六	2,306	四位数以下的英文数字建议直接记阿拉伯数字。
Thirty-two thousand, seven hundred and sixty 三万两千七百六十	32,760	百万以下(简单来讲就是阿拉伯数字中只有一个逗号的)的英文数字可以直接记阿拉伯数字,在听到 thousand 后加逗号辅助。英译中时只要记住逗号前两位是万即可快速输出。
Four hundred and forty thousand, three hundred and twelve 四十四万三百一十二	440,312	
Fifty-six million 五千六百万	56m 56,,	百万及以上的英文数字,可以结合阿拉伯数字和英文单词缩写,如 million、billion 用 m 和 b 代替,或者用一个逗号代表一个段位。英译中时记住关键节点,即靠前的逗号前一位是百万如 9 位数为亿位数,再多一位则为十亿位数。
Nine hundred and seventy-four million, six hundred thousand 九亿七千四百六十万	974m600, 974,600,	

(续表)

数字中英文表达	参考笔记	解析
三万五千 Thirty-five thousand	35,	若记"3 万 5 千",一方面是记录太多,实操时会影响其他信息的记录;另一方面是在记录下来之后还需进一步转化成英文,增加了产出的时间。因此可以在听、记、思环节就将"万"转换为"十千"。
七十五万六千 Seven hundred and fifty-six thousand	756,	几十万的数字,则是在百万下一位,那么就是几百千,可以迅速转换为逗号前三位数。
六百六十万 Six point six million	6.6m	百万数字可以结合 m、小数点和数字快速记录。
九千万 Ninety million	90m	千万和亿是百万位前多一位和两位,即几十 million 和几百 million。
九亿 Nine hundred million	900m	
八十六亿 8.6 billion	8.6b	十亿为 b,结合数字和小数点来记录。

数字口译练习

1. 52,200
2. 320,000
3. 708,000
4. 1,002,000
5. 1,230,000
6. 25,000,000
7. 150,000,000
8. 897,000,000
9. 713,450,000
10. 1,220,000,000
11. 57,000
12. 2,349,000
13. 4,367
14. 122,000
15. 211,211
16. 68,868
17. 68,000
18. 334,000,000
19. 70,100,000,000
20. 888,000,000,000

句子练习

1. **原文**：我们预计今年的营业额为 1.3 亿美元，这将创下公司历史新高。
   参考译文：We expect this year's turnover to be 130 million dollars, which will hit a record high.

2. **原文**：根据最新的市场调查，我们的市场份额增长了八个百分点，达到了 15%。
   参考译文：According to the latest market survey, our market share has increased by 8% points, reaching 15%.

3. **原文**：请尽快与客户联系，确认订单数量为 265 万件，并安排运输事宜。
   参考译文：Please contact the customer as soon as possible to confirm the order quantity of 2.65 million units and arrange the shipment.

4. **原文**：我们的员工数量达到了 54 000 名，我们计划在明年雇用 430 名销售人员和 255 名科研人员，以应对业务的增长需求。
   参考译文：The number of our employees reaches 54,000. We plan to hire 430 new salespeople and 255 researchers next year to meet the growing demands of the business.

5. **原文**：根据最新的财务报表，我们的净利润达到了 280 万美元，超出了预期目标。
   参考译文：According to the latest financial statements, our net profit has reached 2.8 million dollars, exceeding the expected target.

6. **原文**：我们正在与国际合作伙伴商讨一份价值 1 230 万美元的战略合作协议，这将加速我们在海外市场的发展。
   参考译文：We are in discussions with international partners about a strategic cooperation agreement worth 12.3 million dollars, which will accelerate our expansion in overseas markets.

7. **原文**：Our company achieved a 59% sales growth last year, which has given us a significant competitive advantage in the market.

参考译文：我们公司去年实现了59%的销售增长，这使得我们在市场上取得了重要的竞争优势。

8. **原文**：The company reported a revenue of $11.3 million in the last quarter.
   参考译文：公司上个季度报告的收入为1 130万美元。

9. **原文**：The project aims to reduce carbon emissions by 20% within the next five years.
   参考译文：该项目旨在在未来五年内将碳排放降低20%。

10. **原文**：The conference attracted participants from over 50 countries in five continents, totaling more than 1,200 attendees.
    参考译文：该会议吸引了来自五大洲50多个国家的参与者，总计超过1 200名与会者。

11. **原文**：The company's latest investment of $15 million in cutting-edge technology is expected to boost production efficiency by 40% over the next three years.
    参考译文：公司最新投资1 500万美元用于尖端技术，预计在未来3年内将生产效率提高40%。

12. **原文**：The construction of the skyscraper is estimated to cost around $750 million.
    参考译文：这栋摩天大楼的建造估计将花费大约7.5亿美元。

13. **原文**：The government's initiative aims to provide affordable housing for 2 million families by allocating a budget of $3 billion over the course of 10 years.
    参考译文：政府的倡议旨在通过在未来10年内拨款30亿美元，为两百万个家庭提供负担得起的住房。

练习1

Text 1

原文：

Through the U.S. Department of Commerce alone, Puerto Rico will be receiving significant new funding that will help expand opportunity through various programs in Puerto Rico. //

That includes a minimum of $100 million to ensure everyone has access to high-speed internet and the digital skills they need to use that technology and thrive in the digital economy. //

Today, we are excited to announce that Puerto Rico is receiving an initial grant of $5.7 million to plan for the deployment and adoption of high-speed internet across the archipelago. $5 million of this funding will help build out the archipelago's capacity to prepare for our investment and create a plan of action. //

And because we know that internet access is about more than just having a connection, the remaining $700,000 will go toward ensuring that everyone in Puerto Rico has the skills, technology, and capacity they need to take full advantage of our digital economy. //

The money will ensure affordable high-speed internet is available to everyone in Puerto Rico.

To the thousands of small businesses and entrepreneurs across the archipelago, we will provide technical assistance for access to capital through various programs funded by the American Rescue Plan. //

The National Oceanic and Atmospheric Administration will provide more than $7.5 million to support coastal and marine research and education, improve safety in the marine and coastal environment, and ensure sustainable fisheries—all in support of Puerto Rico communities. //

(Adapted from the remarks by Deputy Secretary of Commerce Don Graves at the Puerto Rico Economic Dialogue)

译文：

仅通过美国商务部，波多黎各将获得大量新资金，这将有助于通过波多黎各的各种项目扩大机遇。//

这包括至少1亿美元的资金，以确保每个人都能获得高速互联网以及所需数字技能，以使用技术并在数字经济中蓬勃发展。//

今天，我们很高兴地宣布，波多黎各正在接收第一批570万美元的赠款，用于计划在整个群岛部署和应用高速互联网。这笔资金中的500万美元将用于提高群岛为我们的投资做准备的能力，并制定行动计划。//

因为我们知道拥有互联网不仅仅是拥有连接的可能，所以剩下的70万美元将用于确保波多黎各的每个人都拥有能充分利用我们的数字经济所需的技能、技术和能力。//

这笔钱将确保波多黎各的每个人都能获得负担得起的高速互联网。

对于整个群岛的数千家小企业和企业家，我们将为他们提供技术援助，帮助他们获得美国救援计划资助的各种项目的资金。//

国家海洋和大气管理局（NOAA）将提供750多万美元，以支持沿海和海洋研究和教育，改善海洋和沿海环境的安全，并确保可持续渔业——所有这些都是为了支持波多黎各社区。//

练习解析：

本篇章涉及不少数字，但有部分数字只要在听和思的环节多加处理，便可轻松将其记录下来。例如，本文第三段和第四段提到第一批赠款的数额，以及其分为两部分分别应用于不同方面：570万美元中有500万用于基础能力建设，其余70万用于培养群众相关技能。

Text 2

原文：

帮助外贸企业解决原材料、用工、物流等难题，提升港口集疏运效率，及时回应和解决外资企业关切，货物进出口好于预期，实际使用外资稳定增长。针对就业压力凸显，强化稳岗扩就业政策支持。//

制定实施优化营商环境、市场主体登记管理、促进个体工商户发展、保障中

小企业款项支付等条例。//

改革给人们经商办企业更多便利和空间,去年底企业数量超过5 200万户,个体工商户超过1.1亿户,市场主体总量超过1.6亿户,是十年前的3倍,发展内生动力明显增强。//

推动线上线下消费深度融合,实物商品网上零售额占社会消费品零售总额的比重从15.8%提高到27.2%。//

发展外贸新业态,新设152个跨境电商综试区,支持建设一批海外仓。出台外商投资法实施条例,不断优化外商投资环境。//

对"一带一路"沿线国家货物进出口额年均增长13.4%,各领域交流合作不断深化。//

引导对外投资健康有序发展,加强境外风险防控。//

参考译文:

We assisted foreign trade enterprises in tackling difficulties relating to raw materials, labor, and logistics, improved loading, unloading and transport efficiency in ports, and responded promptly to the concerns of foreign-funded enterprises and helped resolve their problems. The volume of trade in goods exceeded expectations, and utilized foreign investment increased steadily. In response to significant employment pressure, we boosted policy support to stabilize and increase employment. //

We formulated and implemented regulations on improving the business environment, on market entity registration and administration, on promoting development of individually owned businesses, and on ensuring payments to SMEs. //

These reforms have provided people seeking to go into business with greater convenience and scope. By the end of last year, there were over 52 million enterprises and more than 110 million self-employed individuals in China, and the total number of market entities had surpassed the 160-million mark, three times the figure a decade ago. As a result, the internal momentum for development has increased remarkably. //

We vigorously promoted both online and offline consumption, raising the share of online sales for physical goods from 15.8 % to 27.2% of total retail sales of consumer goods. //

We developed new forms of foreign trade, built 152 new integrated pilot zones for cross-border e-commerce, and supported the establishment of overseas warehouses. The regulations for implementing the Foreign Investment Law were issued, further improving the business environment for foreign investors. //

Imports and exports between China and other BRI countries increased at an annual rate of 13.4%, and exchanges and cooperation between China and these countries registered steady progress in a wide range of areas. //

We provided guidance which ensured sound and orderly development of outbound investment, and we strengthened overseas risk prevention and control. //

练习解析：

每年的政府工作报告都是很好的翻译练习素材。由于其内容丰富、涉及知识面广，对译员的知识储备和双语水平都提出了很高的要求。

本段材料涉及过去一年国家在商务、经贸领域的工作。数字较多，信息量大，需积极调动储备，同时做好笔记，尤其是记录数字对应的含义。

注意"提高到"和"提高了"的不同表达，如文中"从15.8%提高到27.2%"应为"raise... from... to...,"而"增长13.4%"则应为"increase by 13.4%"或"increase at a rate of 13.4%"。

同时，要多积累同一词汇不同的译法，如增减在英文中就有针对不同程度的词汇：

增（↑）	减（↓）
increase	reduce
go up	decrease
rocket up	lower
raise/rise	fall
expand	drop
enlarge	dwindle
build up	cut
skyrocket	shorten
spike	slash
…	…

请注意，口译过程中既要表达多样化，即同一个词用不同的方式表达，也要注意不同词汇的搭配及表达方式的区别，不可滥用，确保用词准确。

练习 2

Dialogue 1

原文：

A: 你好，欧女士。我叫邹晓，是来自深圳春风牛奶公司的采购经理。

B: Hello, Ms. Zou, I'm very glad to see you. I'm the sales manager from the New Zealand Pastoral Milk Supply Company.

A: 我们已经看过贵公司发给我们的相关产品的价格。但是很遗憾价格远远超过了我们的预算，所以我想商量一下怎么达成一个我们双方都能接受的价格。

B: OK, I'm open to discussion. Our quotation is quite competitive, and already includes a 5% discount. You might find a supplier with a lower cost, but that could compromise on quality.

A: 感谢您的折扣。我确实比较喜欢你们的牛奶，口感好，奶味浓。但是您方的报价是 40 元一箱。为了达成合作，我们希望价格能降到 28 元。

B: That's an extra 30% discount, which is a big ask. I can offer 35 per case, but that would be on the condition that you order 15,000 cases. And the turnaround time is two months.

A: 好的，这样吧，你们能不能给到每箱牛奶32元，周转时间5周呢？我们可以订购2万箱牛奶。如果可以，我今天就授权下单。在接下来的几个月我们会订购很多这样的产品。我希望能和一家供应商建立强有力的合作关系。

B: OK deal. But you should know, these few months are our peak order seasons. We still have a lot of back orders on hand. It's very difficult to do it as you expect. We will complete your order in as soon as seven weeks.

A: 但是我们现在在国内的库存已经开始紧张了，我们很需要这笔订单的货物来填补仓库缺口。你们能在6周内就给我们供货吗？

B: Yes, I know. You don't have to worry too much. We are also working on expediting the order. we will definitely give priority to your order concerning delivery. We will try to complete the shipment within six weeks.

A: 没问题。再次感谢你们的配合。期待未来能再次和你们合作。

B: Thank you for your understanding. We look forward to a pleasant cooperation with you!

参考译文：

A: Hello, Ms. Ou. I'm Zou Xiao, purchasing manager from Shenzhen Chunfeng Milk Company.

B: 你好，邹女士，很高兴见到你。我是来自新西兰田园牛奶供应公司的销售经理。

A: We have reviewed the quote of the products from your company. Unfortunately, the price exceeds our budget, so I'd like to discuss how to reach a price that works for both of us.

B: 没问题，这个可以商量。我们给出的报价是非常有竞争力的，而且已经打了九五折了。你也许能找到一个成本更低的供应商，但质量就会打折扣。

A: Thank you for the discount. I do appreciate your milk with its good flavor and creamy taste. But your quotation is 40 yuan per case. We want to make the deal by setting the price at 28 yuan per case.

B: 这就要额外打七折了，这个要求可不低。我可以给你算 35 元一箱，但是条件是要订购 1.5 万箱。产品准备周期是两个月。

A: OK. How about 32 yuan per case and five weeks of turnaround? We can order 20,000 cases of milk. If possible, I will authorize the order today. We will have more orders in the next few months. I would like to work in strong partnership with one supplier.

B: 好的，成交，但是你们知道的，这几个月是我们的订单高峰期。我们还有很多即将过期的订单还没处理好。要按照你们的期望，这很难做到。我们最快用 7 周完成您的订单。

A: Our domestic stock is running low, and we urgently need this order to replenish our inventory. Can you supply us with the goods in six weeks?

B: 我知道我知道。你们可以放心。我们也有在对订单进行加急处理，肯定会优先为贵公司安排发货。我们尽量在 6 周内完成装运。

A: No problem. Thanks again for your cooperation. I'm looking forward to working with you again in the future.

B: 感谢贵公司的理解。希望合作愉快！

练习解析：

本对话练习中的数值并不大，不难记录。但千万不要因为记录数字而忘记记录数字所对应的文本信息。例如，"That's an extra 30% discount, which is a big ask. I can do 35 per unit, but that would be on the condition that you order 15,000 cases. And the turnaround time is two months."这一个语段中共有四个数字，笔记不仅需记下数字，还要记下数字分别代表的含义。

值得一提的是，折扣的表达在中文和英文中有差异。英文通常表达为百分之几的折扣（percentage discount），但中文一般不说百分之几的折扣，而是说几折。例如，30% discount 是七折，5% discount 是九五折。

Dialogue 2

原文：

A: 您好，我是国际名酒展览会的展会负责人，请问有什么能为您服务的呢？

B: Hello, I am Mumm wine merchant representative Mok. I would like to present my products at your exhibition. Can you give me some information about your bare booth costs and conditions?

A: 当然，光地展位36平方米起订，产品展区每平方米1 600元。需要您自行搭建展台。

B: I think the cost of your booth is a bit steep. Can I have a discount?

A: 因为您是第一次参加我们的展会，我们可以根据您的展位面积和位置给你一些折扣。

B: That's great, I'd like a booth near the entrance, about 40 square meters. What kind of discount can you give me?

A: 我们的展位是按照区域划分的，靠近入口的展位属于A区。我们在A区的展位还有几个空位，您可以选择一个喜欢的位置。我们可以给你九三折，这是我们的最低价了。

B: Well, I can agree to that price. Well, can you also do some promotional work for us before the show starts?

A: 好的，我们会通过媒体帮你们做一定的宣传。我们的展览是很有影响力和专业性的，你会得到很多潜在的客户和合作伙伴。

B: That's great. I'm pleased to have reached an agreement with you. May I ask what other necessary formalities I need to complete now?

A: 这边需要您填写一份展位申请表，然后签署一份展位合同。您可以在我们官网上找到您需要的资料和我们的电子邮箱地址。

B: Okay, I will send the documents to you as soon as possible. Thank you for your help and look forward to working with you.

A: 不客气，我们也很高兴能与您合作。如果您有任何问题，可以随时联系我们。

参考译文：

A: Good day, I am the manager of the International Wine Exhibition. How can I help you?

B: 您好，我是玛姆酒商代表人Mok，我想在你们的展览上展示我的产品，能向我介绍一下你们的光地展位费用和条件吗？

A: Of course. Bare booth is available from 36 square meters and 1,600 yuan per square meter at the product area. You'll need to build your own stand.

B: 我觉得你们的展位费用有点高，能不能给我一些优惠呢？

A: As this is your first time attending our exhibition, we can offer you some discounts depending on the size and location of your stand.

B: 那太好了，我想要一个靠近入口的展位，面积大概是40平方米，您能给我多少折扣呢？

A: Our booths are divided into different parts and the booths near the entrance belong to Area A. We still have a few booths available in area A. You can choose one that you like. We can give you a 7% discount, which is our lowest price.

B: 好吧，这个价格我可以接受，另外，在展会开始前你们能够帮我们做些宣传工作吗？

A: Of course. We will help you advertise through the media. Our exhibitions are very influential and professional, and you will get many potential customers and partners.

B: 那太好了，我很高兴能和你们达成协议。请问我现在还需要完成什么必要手续呢？

A: Here you will need to fill in a booth application form and sign a booth contract. You can find the information you need and our email address on our website.

B: 好的，我尽快把文件发给您。谢谢您的帮助，期待与你们合作。

A: You're welcome, and we're also delighted to work with you. If you have any questions, don't hesitate to contact us.

练习解析：

口译最重要的就是将原文信息传达出去，如果在口译中一时找不到准确对应的词，不要长时间停顿，换一种表达方式，将意思讲明即可。例如"九三折"换一种表达方式即为7%的折扣，英文为"7% discount"；又如文中的"宣传"，你是否会在口译时在想"宣传"到底用哪个词？如果一直纠结于此，必定会造成口译不顺畅，出现大段空白。其实，换个思路想想，为产品做宣传就是打广告，即advertise (v.)，或do some promotional work，也可以用"promote our products"。

Dialogue 3

原文：

A: Hello. I'm Rachel. Nice to meet you. Thank you for taking the time to meet with me today.

B: 你好，Rachel女士。我是陈明。我是深圳科技公司的总经理。首先，我会给你介绍一下我们公司的生产线。

A: Thank you. Are all your production lines fully automated?

B: 并不是全自动的。但我们的技术是行业内领先的。

A: I see. How do you ensure quality control, then?

B: 所有产品在整个生产过程中都必须通过五道质量检查关。

A: What is the monthly production output, may I ask?

B: 目前工厂每月生产 1 168 套配件，但从八月份开始每月将提高为 1 579 套。

A: If we place an order now, how long will it take for delivery?

B: 那要看订单大小以及你需要的产品而定。

A: What is the average monthly defect rate?

B: 正常情况下为 2.1% 左右。我们的实验表明这种型号至少可以使用 51 260 小时。这比在它的价格范围内的任何其他型号都要高出 1.1 万小时左右。

A: That's great to hear. However, what should we do in case the equipment malfunctions during our use?

B: 一旦发生那样的情况，同我们最近的办事处联系，他们会马上派人过去的。

A: I understand. Mr. Chen, another purpose of my visit is to explore the possibility of establishing a long-term business relationship with your company. We are primarily interested in the scale of your company, product range, operational procedures and financial status.

B: 你方想与我方建立长期业务关系的愿望与我方是一致的，但是我对贵公司并不是很了解，烦请给我们做一下介绍。

A: Indeed, you can verify our financial status, creditworthiness, and reputation with the Bank of China's New York Branch or the local Chamber of Commerce.

B: 感谢你方提供的信息。我相信我们之间建立业务关系将对双方都有利。

A: This is my first visit to your company. I'd appreciate your support and cooperation in our upcoming negotiations.

B: 我们十分乐意提供支持，也一定会全力配合。

参考译文：

A: 你好，我是 Rachel。很高兴见到你，谢谢你们今天抽出时间与我会面。

B: Hello, Ms. Rachel. I'm Chen Ming. I am the General Manager of Shenzhen Technology Company. First, I'd like to provide you with an overview of our company's production line.

A: 谢谢。你们的生产线都是全自动的吗？

B: It's not entirely automated, but our technology is industry-leading.

A: 我知道了，那你们如何控制质量呢？

B: All products must pass through five quality inspection checkpoints throughout the entire production process.

A: 请问月产量是多少呢？

B: Currently, the factory produces 1,168 sets of components per month, but starting from August, the monthly production will increase to 1,579 sets.

A: 如果我们现在订货，到交货前需要多长时间呢？

B: The lead time for delivery will depend on the size of the order and the specific products you require.

A: 请问每月的不良率通常是多少？

B: Typically, it's around 2.1%. Our testing indicates this model can last at least 51,260 hours, which is about 11,000 hours more than any other model in its price range.

A: 非常好。不过如果这种设备在我们使用的时候发生故障该怎么办呢？

B: If that were to happen, please contact our nearest office, and they will promptly send someone to assist.

A: 我明白了。陈先生，我此行另一个目的是想探询与贵公司建立长期业务关系的可能性。我们主要对贵公司的规模、产品范围、运作流程和财务状况感兴趣。

B: Your desire to establish a long-term business relationship aligns with our intentions. However, I'm not very familiar with your company. Could you please provide us with an introduction?

A: 其实，关于我们的财务状况、信用度和声誉，都可向中国银行纽约分行或当地商会咨询了解。

B: Thank you for providing this information. I believe that establishing a business relationship between us will be mutually beneficial.

A: 这是我初次拜访贵公司，在接下来的洽谈中还请多加支持配合。

B: We are more than willing to support and assure you of our full cooperation.

练习解析：

原文多为短句，便于记忆和翻译。其中出现的数字需重点记忆，并注意区分和读法。比如 51 260 和 1.1 万转换成英语，应记录为 51,260 和 11,000。此外，汉语中"左右、大约、大概、将近"等修饰不确定数字的词语在英语中，可使用"about, around, nearly, towards, somewhere about, estimated, approximately, close to"等词来表示，可使用约等于号"≈"。"高出……小时"不能直译成"... hours higher than"，应选择适用于描述时间的"longer than"或"more than"。

第 5 单元

增译与减译

我们在第 1 单元提过，口译要做到"达意"，即准确传达源语的意思，抓住实质意义。译员在口译时往往并不用字对字译出，而应在表达上更为灵活，因此常用到增译或减译技巧。

5.1 增译法

增译技巧普遍运用于汉英翻译。根据英汉语言习惯的不同，增译主要包含以下方法：

5.1.1 增主语

从语言学的角度来看，英语是主语突出的语言，而汉语是主题突出的语言，也可称为零主语。汉语句子有时会缺乏明确的主语。因此除非源语英语是一个"零主语"的句子，或者使用了被动语态或"There be"句型，否则在进行汉英翻译时，建议增加主语。

5.1.2 增代词、连词等

英语和汉语在名词、代词、连词、介词、冠词等的用法上存在较大差异。英语常用代词，按照英语语法，指代人时须在名词前使用物主代词，表示某人或某物之间的所属关系。因此，在进行汉英翻译时，需要在译文中相应地增加物主代词。在英语中连词是体现名词、从句和句子之间逻辑关系的关键，而汉语中的逻辑关系则一般通过上下文和语序来体现。因此，汉译英时不可避免地需要补充连词，使上下文更加连贯、通顺。

5.1.3 增加解释性语言

当出现目的语文化背景中无法理解、即使译入目的语也无法让受众明白的内容时，口译员往往需要增加必要的解释性词句，但应避免偏离原文核心内容。

句子精练

1. **原文**：各地区各部门增强"四个意识"、坚定"四个自信"、做到"两个维护"。

参考译文：All localities and government departments <u>enhanced their consciousness of the need to maintain political integrity, think in big-picture terms, follow the leadership core, and keep in alignment with the central Party leadership; stayed confident in the path, theory, system, and culture of socialism with Chinese characteristics; upheld Comrade Xi Jinping's core position on the Party Central Committee and in the Party as a whole, and upheld the Central Committee's authority and its centralized, unified leadership.</u>

解析：由于英语的受众群体对原文中的"四个意识""四个自信"和"两个维护"缺乏一定的背景了解，因此采用增译方法，增加了解释性的文字，即对应的具体内容。当然，在口译过程中也需要考虑口译时长，如在同声传译或议程较赶的交替传译的情况下，则应适当缩减增译内容。

2. **原文**：We fully leveraged China's super-sized market and carried out the strategy of expanding domestic demand to foster more growth engines.

   参考译文：我们立足超大规模市场<u>优势</u>，坚持实施扩大内需战略，培育更多经济增长动力源。

   解析：在将"We fully leveraged China's super-sized market"翻译成中文时，译者添加"advantage"（优势）一词，可以使翻译更加完整。在翻译特定文化语境下的词汇或表达时，增译的重要性在于它提供了额外的解释来帮助不熟悉源语言文化的读者更好地理解原文。

5.2 减译法

减译法是指"当译文中虽无其词而已有其意，或者在译文中不言而喻，则原文中这些词在译文中便可不译出来"[1]。例如，为了保持语法结构的完整性，英语中经常使用介词，而中文往往简明扼要。因此在英汉翻译过程中，可以减去介词或翻译成动词。

---

[1] 郭著章，李庆生，刘军平. 2010. 英汉互译实用教程. 武汉：武汉大学出版社.

此外，减译法也可理解为词的省略，对于语义上重复、冗余或不符合于目的语的语言习惯的用词都可省略，但不应影响原文中心思想。在商务口译中，为确保在短时间内快速准确地传达讲者的意图，也可基于此原则采取减译法。

句子精练

1. **原文**：坚持绿水青山就是金山银山的理念。

   参考译文：Stay true to the idea that lucid waters and lush mountains are invaluable assets.

   解析：原文中的"金山银山"无法找到准确且对应的目的语翻译，如果译为"Golden Mountain and Silver Mountain"则会使目的语受众感到困惑，难以理解句子真正的含义。因此，建议采取减译法，抓住其核心意思，并将其翻译成"invaluable assets"。

2. **原文**：A psychology study reveals that people tend to lose their temper with someone they know over those they are not familiar with.

   参考译文：一项心理研究表明，人往往倾向于和熟悉的人发脾气。

   解析：这句译文中省略了 over those they are not familiar with "比起他们不熟悉的人"。中文是一门言简意赅的语言，译文表达应干净利索不拖沓，否则会显得冗长啰唆。

 5.3 口译练习

练习 1

Text 1

本文是深圳技术大学阮双琛校长在 2019 年 5 月高桌晚宴上的致辞。请先预习词汇，听录音，并进行带笔记交传。录音已分割为多个语段，请在提示音后暂停录音并开始口译。

词汇预习

深圳技术大学	Shenzhen Technology University (SZTU)
中华人民共和国成立70周年	the 70th anniversary of the People's Republic of China
十八大	the 18th National Congress of the Communist Party of China
总书记	General Secretary of the CPC Central Committee
立德树人	morality education
德智体美劳全面发展	all-round moral, intellectual, physical, and aesthetical grounding with a hard-working spirit
高桌晚宴	High Table Dinner
巴伐利亚之夜	Bavarian Night
高水平应用技术大学国际论坛	International Forum on High Level Universities of Applied Sciences

Text 2

本文是深圳技术大学商学院荣誉院长 Holger Haldenwang 在 2020 年 9 月开学典礼上的演讲致辞。请先预习词汇，听录音，并进行带笔记交传。录音已分割为多个语段，请在提示音后暂停录音并开始口译。

词汇预习

欢迎辞	welcome address
巴伐利亚州	federal state Bavaria
具有前瞻性、实践性和产业导向性的教育	future-looking, hands-on and industry-oriented education
校企合作	university-company cooperation

练习 2

Dialogue 1

四人小组对话口译练习，两人为讲者，两人为译员。当然，你也可以通过扫码进行自主练习，在提示音后进行口译。

词汇预习

农夫山泉	Nongfu Spring
批发商	distributor
数量不符	quantity discrepancy
转运	transit
离岸价	FOB (free on board)
船运公司	shipping company
提出索赔	lodge/file a claim with...

Dialogue 2

四人小组对话口译练习，可互换讲者和译员角色。同样，你也可以进行自主练习。

词汇预习

业绩	performance
研发	R&D (research and development)
产能	production capacity
互信	mutual trust
共赢	win-win
长期稳定关系	long-term and stable relationalship

Dialogue 3

四人小组对话口译练习,自选讲者和译员角色。同样,你也可以进行自主练习。

词汇预习

出口部经理	Export Manager
产品目录	product
贸易公司	trading company
进出口经营权	import and export rights

5.4 练习原文、译文及解析

练习 1

Text 1

原文:

各位嘉宾,各位朋友,先生们、女士们:

大家晚上好!

今年是庆祝中华人民共和国成立70周年。在这个特殊时刻,我们相聚于此隆重举行深圳技术大学高桌晚宴,共同感受西方礼仪带来的文化盛宴。// 在此我仅代表深圳技术大学对各位嘉宾、朋友及师生们的到来表示衷心感谢和热烈欢迎。通过今晚的盛宴,相信大家必将在此度过一个愉快而又美好的夜晚。//

培养什么人?怎样培养人?是深圳高校普遍思考和关注的核心问题。党的十八大以来,习总书记曾多次强调高校立身之本在于立德树人,国无德不兴,人无德不立,只有培养出一流人才的高校,才能够成为世界一流的大学。//

建校以来，深圳技术大学始终牢记立德树人使命，培养学生"先做人，再成才"。学校在学科规划、专业设置、师生交流、人才培养等方面，注重中西结合，不断深化和巩固中外合作办学的新模式、新成果，全力培养德智体美劳全面发展的社会主义建设者和接班人。//

同学们，你们要知道，深圳技术大学是一所没有围墙、开放式的大学，拥护文化多样性和全球化视野。因此，大家必须睁大双眼看世界，高瞻远瞩。大家将与来自五湖四海的人交流，应敢于探索科学和知识的边界。请将整座城市，乃至整个世界，作为迎风敞开的课堂，探索未知的世界，和社会融为一体，而非自我封闭。// 因此，三年多来，我们始终坚持定期举办国际周活动，同期举办高桌晚宴、巴伐利亚之夜、高水平应用技术大学国际论坛，力求为同学们创造一个拓宽视野、增长知识的平台，营造一个开放包容、求实进取的学习氛围。//

同学们，本次国际周共40余名教授开设129门课程，希望你们珍惜机会，认真交流，虚心学习，培养专业兴趣，为以后4年大学学习奠定基础。

最后，祝所有嘉宾、2019级新生度过一个愉快而又难忘的夜晚！

谢谢大家！//

参考译文：

Distinguished guests, dear friends, ladies and gentlemen:

Good evening!

This year marks the 70th anniversary of the People's Republic of China. Tonight, we gather here in this High Table Dinner to experience the western culture. // First, please allow me, on behalf of Shenzhen Technology University to extend my sincere gratitude and warm welcome to all of you. I believe you will have a pleasant and beautiful evening. //

What kind of talents we shall nurture? And how can we achieve that? These are the two core issues facing all universities in Shenzhen. Since the 18th National Congress of the Communist Party of China, Xi Jinping, General Secretary of the CPC Central Committee, has stressed many times that the foundation of a university is to cultivate students with not only knowledge, but also virtue. A country cannot prosper without virtues, nor can anyone succeed without virtues. World-class universities only refer to those who produce top level talents. //

From the very beginning, SZTU has kept in mind the morality education by cultivating students to be decent before being successful. SZTU gives priority to a combination of Eastern and Western education in disciplinary planning, curriculum development, teacher/student exchanges and talent cultivation. We deepen and enhance the new models and achievements in Chinese-foreign cooperation in running schools, striving to foster a new generation of young people who have all-round moral, intellectual, physical, and aesthetical grounding with a hard-working spirit. //

Dear students of 2019, you shall understand that SZTU is an open university without walls. We embrace cultural diversity and global perspective. Therefore, you have to open your eyes to the world, think wide and high. You will need to communicate with people from diverse backgrounds. You shall dare to explore boundaries of sciences and knowledge. Embrace the entire city and the world as your classroom, venturing into the unknown. Get involved into the society rather than be isolated. // That's why we organize International Week for you. It includes colorful events like the High Table Dinner, Bavarian Night, and International Forum on High Level Universities of Applied Sciences. I hope it will help you broaden your horizon, enrich understanding of knowledge. We aim to create an open, inclusive, pragmatic and enterprising environment for you to study and live. //

Dear freshmen, over forty senior professors have offered 129 courses specifically for you. Please cherish this unique opportunity, and be humble and respect knowledge. More importantly, please try to find your interest in your majors. I hope it could lay a sound foundation for the next four years of study.

Finally, ladies and gentlemen, I wish this High Table Dinner a great success! Enjoy your night!

Thank you very much! //

练习解析：

在汉译英中，当涉及中国特色词汇或者特定背景下产生的习语和俗语时，要在译文中增加解释性语言，让目的语的听众能更了解原文的内容和含义。原文"国无德不兴，人无德不立"中的"德"指人的品德，"兴"是国家的繁荣昌盛，"立"在本场景下指的则是一个人的成功，此句可译为"A country cannot prosper without virtues, nor can anyone succeed without virtues"；在"先做人，再成才"中，"做人"结合前文"立德树人使命"，意为"做品德优良的人"，可译为"cultivating students to be a decent citizen / a man of great moral integrity"或"cultivating students to be decent"，"成才"则是指取得成功。因此，无论是英译汉还是汉译英，都要注重信息的客观传递，确保译文的语义完整，且目标语群体能够获得与源语群体相同的信息。译员需要充分了解英语和汉语两种语言的特点，熟练运用增译法和减译法，在保证与讲者的主题内容和话语逻辑一致的前提下，根据两种语言的表达特点，灵活调整句式表达。

Text 2

原文：

Dear students, dear colleagues, nihao, hello. First, I'm glad that we met as scheduled in this beautiful campus. Today, I'd like to extend a warm welcome to the new students! Welcome to Shenzhen Technology University! //

Your arrival makes this university full of vigor and vitality. I am addressing you today after being isolated for the last 14 days after my arrival on 12th September in Guangzhou, and I didn't become crazy, because I intended to give this welcome address. //

2020 is an extraordinary and challenging year. This still existing Corona crisis presents us all with a task of historic proportions. These are restrictions such as have never been seen before in the Federal Republic of Germany. //

Universities, schools and kindergartens are working with some restrictions like online-teaching, wearing masks, part-time lock downs, social contacts reduced to a minimum, those who can, work in the home office. //

A lot of major events have been cancelled, and border crossings sometimes are closed. The past six months have been marked by great challenges and completely new life situations for all of us. //

We have faced up to the tasks, both professionally and privately, and tried to cope with the uncertainties as best we could. We have taken care to influence the situation in a positive sense—as far as possible—through our actions. //

I am firmly convinced that we all gave our best as members of this wonderful university. And I think we made purposeful and level-headed decisions, and thus mastered the challenges in the team very well. //

Although the crisis has not yet been overcome, I am sure that we will continue to coordinate, plan and execute the coming semester in the best possible way for all members of the SZTU. //

Please allow me to reemphasize the SZTU's sparkling characteristics, the Germany-inspired concept of Applied Sciences. I come from Regensburg, compared to Shenzhen a small, but more than two thousand years old city, located in the middle of the federal state Bavaria. //

I am very intimate with this "applied" model of learning as I have spent my entire academic career, which is now almost 35 years at the University of Applied Sciences in Regensburg. //

Thus, I have seen first-hand, and feel very proud of, this model of educational philosophy. Why am I so proud? After seeing generations and generations of students graduating from our University, finding jobs quickly and, thereafter, successfully advancing their careers, I can say that this model offers an incomparable future-looking, hands-on and industry-oriented education to build the next generation of leaders. //

Dear students, be always prepared to make a good use of upcoming opportunities.

As an applied sciences university, we are characterized by enormous overseas exchange programs and compulsory internships in companies. You will have many opportunities to go abroad during your study. // Up to now, before the Corona crises stopped this, students of SZTU already had 14 trips, Germany, Switzerland and even the USA to join the Summer/Springtime/Winter schools. Also, you will also face many chances for interns in companies, especially the opening of SZTU overseas liaison offices in Germany will boost future company-university cooperation in the future. //

Please understand beforehand that the education of future engineers and business men has to include the practice in enterprises. As the saying goes, practice makes perfect, especially, around five to six months lasting internships arranged are very important for gaining subjects to the later Bachelor and Master thesis. //

Please bear me to reemphasize that a good command of major-related expertise, German and English language will make you stand out when applying for those overseas exchange programs and internships, and those valuable experience gained from these can enhance your employability and offer you an incomparable capability to become the next generation of leaders. //

But you must think that in every new situation there are some obstacles you must overcome, and believe me, don't be afraid to face challenges, learn to be strong and confident.

As long as you don't give in when you are frustrated, success must belong to you! //

Later on in your life you will be very proud to say, I was within the first groups of graduates at the famous SZTU, and especially within a new type of university of applied sciences.

Last but not least, my dear students, before I come to the end, I'd like to underline the following thoughts. I know to study in a university means a little freedom, not to be under permanent control by the parents, and of course to have fun as well and will celebrate parties, or other great things. //

But on the other side I request you to be engaged in study and the university community, take care of the others and respect the others. //

And please protect the environment too. Throw your waste in the garbage and try to separate glass, metal, plastic, paper and others. //

I would like to end my welcome address with a small quote, "To stay positive does not mean that things will always work out. Rather, it's known that you'll be okay no matter how things turn out."

I wish us all to stay healthy and positive!

Thank you!//

参考译文：

亲爱的同学们，同事们，大家好！首先，很高兴我们能如期在这个美丽的校园相遇。今天，我要向所有的新生表示热烈的欢迎！欢迎来到深圳技术大学！//

你们的到来让校园充满生机和活力。9月12日抵达广州后，我在酒店被集中隔离了14天，但一想到今天要来致开学欢迎辞，我的内心充满期待。//

2020年是个非同寻常、充满挑战的一年。这场新冠疫情向我们所有人提出了一项历史性挑战，比如德国采取了前所未有的限制措施。//

一些大学、中学和幼儿园都改成线上教学，还有出门要戴口罩，时不时地封锁，社交活动大幅度减少和居家办公。//

许多重大活动被取消，边境口岸有时也关闭。过去六个月里，我们面临巨大的挑战和全新的生活环境。//

无论是工作还是生活，我们都勇敢面对这些挑战，并尽全力应对各种不确定因素。我们尽其所能地采取行动积极应对这种局势。//

我坚信，今天大家能坐在这里，一定是付出了巨大的努力。我们果断、清晰地做出各种决定，从而也完美地应对团队中的各项困难。//

即使疫情还未结束，但我相信我们会继续以最好的状态，协调、计划和开展

这一学期的工作。//

在这里，请允许我再次强调一下深圳技术大学的示范性特色——受德国启发的应用技术型办学理念。我来自德国雷根斯堡市，与深圳相比，雷根斯堡是一个有两千多年历史的小城市，位于巴伐利亚州中部。//

我非常熟悉这种"应用型"教育模式，因为我在德国雷根斯堡应用技术大学，度过了将近35年的学术生涯。//

我亲眼见证这种教育模式的实践成果并为此感到非常自豪。为什么呢？看到一批又一批的学生从我们的大学毕业后，迅速找到工作，然后成功地步入职场。我可以说，这种模式在培养下一代商业领袖方面具有无与伦比的前瞻性、实践性和产业导向性。//

亲爱的同学们，请时刻准备好迎接即将到来的机会。

作为一所应用技术型大学，我们学校有丰富的海外交流项目和实习机会，在校期间还会有很多出国交流的机会。// 到目前为止，疫情发生之前，深圳技术大学的学生已前往德国、瑞士、美国等国家参加过14场夏令营、春令营以及冬令营。此外，还有许多去知名企业实习的机会，深圳技术大学在德国设立的海外办公室，未来也将促进企业与大学的合作。//

要知道，未来的工程师和企业家必须有丰富的企业实战经验。俗话说，熟能生巧，五到六个月左右的实习时间，对于以后撰写学士和硕士学位论文非常重要。//

请允许我再次强调一下，熟练掌握相关专业知识、学好德语和英语能让你在申请海外交流项目和实习时脱颖而出，从中获取的宝贵经验可以提高你的就业能力，赋予你无可比拟的才能，为成为下一代商业领袖做好准备。//

但是你必须知道，无论在什么情况下都需要克服各种困难。相信我，不要害怕面对挑战，学会坚强和自信。

沮丧的时候不屈服，成功就一定属于你！//

往后你会很自豪地说：我是著名的深圳技术大学的第一批毕业生！而且还是一所新型的应用技术型大学！

最后，亲爱的同学们，结束之前，我还想强调以下几点：我知道上了大学之后比较自由了，父母也不再管着你了，当然会有很多有趣的事，会参加各种聚会，或其他重大的活动。//

但另一方面，我希望你们能认真学习，积极参加大学社团，照顾他人，尊重他人。//

也请爱护环境，做好垃圾分类。把玻璃、金属、塑料、纸和其他东西尽量合理分类处理。//

最后，我想用一句话结束今天的致辞，"乐观未必常如意，柳暗花明会有时"。

祝大家身体健康，乐观向上！

谢谢！//

练习解析：

英译汉中需要特别注意提取关键逻辑信息，删减冗余，确保译文简洁到位。原文"To stay positive does not mean that things will always work out. Rather, it's known that you'll be okay no matter how things turn out."的中心思想是鼓励人们就算面对逆境，也要时刻保持乐观心态，用词较口语化，不易将所有的衔接词都直译成汉语。面对这种鼓励性质的词句，可以考虑翻译成脍炙人口的诗句、习语、俗语。在这个情境下将原文翻译成"乐观未必常如意，柳暗花明会有时"更能体现汉语言简意赅的语言特色和独特的文化底蕴。

练习 2

Dialogue 1

原文：

A: 您好！我是此次农夫山泉系列产品的批发商之一，我是蔡经理。欢迎您的来访。请问有什么我可以帮到您？

B: It's a pleasure to meet you. I must bring up an unfortunate issue during our conversation today.

A: 好的，您请讲，我们会尽力为您提供一个合适的解决方案。

B: It's about the drinks we bought here last time. We inspected and counted the goods as soon as they arrived. To our disappointment, we found that the quantity was significantly different from that on the order. Here are the records from the last count. You can have a look at them by yourself.

A: 听到这一消息我们感到很遗憾。这批货物装船时已进行多次清点，是确定数量无误才出发的。你们找出产品数量不符的原因了吗？

B: We believe that the quantity of Nongfu Spring drinks we received is seriously inconsistent with the order because the inventory was not correctly counted during the shipment.

A: 不可能。你知道我们的订单协议已严格要求数量清点。我们怀疑这次的问题很可能是在转运时丢失所导致的。

B: We've incurred losses due to the missing batch of goods. I'm looking for a solution to address these losses. Do you have any reasonable plan?

A: 是这样的，这批饮品订单是以离岸价成交的。在签订协议时我们共同协商我方不负责运输，船运公司全程由您方联系，且保险也是由您方自己承担。我方的建议是您方可以先向船运公司调查情况，或向保险公司提出索赔。如果后续需要我们为您提供证据，我方一定会全力支持。

B: Understood, we'll consider your recommendation. However, I hope you can send someone to follow the case up. Should any issues arise, I'll get in touch immediately.

A: 对你们遭受的损失我深表同情。我希望在今后的交易中一切顺利。

B: I hope so.

参考译文：

A: Hello! I am Manager Cai, one of the distributors of the Nongfu Spring series products. Welcome! What can I do for you?

B: 您好！今天来找您，是有件非常不愉快的事要与您谈。

A: OK, go ahead. We'll try our best to provide you with a suitable solution.

B: 是关于我们上次在这里购买的一批饮品。货物运抵之后，我们马上对其进行了检查及清点。令我们失望的是，我们发现其数量与订单上的严重不符。这是上次我们清点的数据记录，您可以看一下。

A: We're sorry to hear that. Please know that before shipping, we thoroughly counted the goods multiple times to ensure accuracy. Have you found out the reason for the quantity discrepancy?

B: 我们认为是在装船时清点工作不到位导致的。

A: No way. You know our order agreement has strict requirements for quantity counting. This problem is probably caused by loss in transit.

B: 这批丢失的货物已经给我方造成了损失，我现在需要的是一个能够弥补损失的解决方案。您方有什么合理的方案吗？

A: Well, the order for drinks is placed on FOB basis. At the time of signing the agreement, we agreed that our party would not be responsible for the transportation. The shipping company shall be contacted by your side throughout the whole process and the insurance shall be arranged by you as well. Our suggestion is that you can first make an inquiry with the shipping company or lodge a claim with the insurance company. If evidence is needed from our side later, we will give full support.

B: 行吧，我们会采纳您的建议。但我希望您方能派人跟进一下，一旦有问题我会立即与您方沟通的。

A: I'm very sorry for your loss. I wish all the best in our future dealings.

B: 希望如此。

练习解析：

在商务对话口译中，要结合上下文语境，当源语发言重复或冗余时，应采取减译策略，保证译文简洁。例如，"We believe that <u>the quantity of Nongfu Spring drinks we received is seriously inconsistent with the order</u> because the inventory was not correctly counted during the shipment."中的画线内容在上文已经出现过，可以不译出，直接将整句译为"我们认为是……造成的"即可。又如，"I hope you can send someone to follow the case up."中的"the case"可不译出，因为根据上下文语境，中方人员非常清楚要跟进的是什么事情，直接译为"派人跟进一下"则更符合中文口语的习惯和简洁性。

Dialogue 2

原文：

A: 您好，欢迎来到中国。我是本公司的代表，很高兴见到您。

B: Hello, I am a business representative from the United States. It is my honor to come to China to meet you.

A: 非常感谢您的到来。

B: We have heard that your company has a very influential position in the Chinese market. We would like to know your business situation and development plan.

A: 非常感谢您的关注。我们是一家致力于提供高品质产品和服务的公司，专注于化学工业的研发和销售，已经在中国市场取得了不错的业绩。我们的发展规划是拓展国际市场，希望能够与您合作。

B: We are also very interested in cooperating with you. We hope to cooperate with you in technology and to research and develop new products.

A: 我们非常注重技术创新和研发，并且拥有一支优秀的研发团队，可以与您合作共同开发新产品。同时，我们还注重产品质量和服务，可以帮助您在中国市场销售您的产品。

B: Sounds great. We'd also like to know your production capacity and plant equipment.

A: 我们有一些先进的生产设备和生产线，可以保证产品的质量和效率。如果您有兴趣的话，我们可以带您参观我们的工厂。

B: Thank you very much. We would be happy to learn about your production equipment and factory. And what are your company's cooperation methods?

A: 我们的合作方式非常灵活，可以根据您的需求和要求制定合适的合作方案。我们可以讨论合作方式、时间以及产品等具体的细节。我们非常注重合作过程中的互信和共赢，希望能够与您建立长期稳定的合作关系。

B: We also strongly agree with the concept of mutual trust and win-win cooperation. We hope to establish long-term and stable cooperative relations with common development.

A: 我们非常期待与您建立合作关系。如果您有任何问题或需要进一步了解，请随时联系我们。

B: Thank you very much, we will.

参考译文：

A: Hello, welcome to China. I am the representative of our company. Nice to meet you.

B: 您好，我是来自美国的商务代表，很荣幸来到中国和您会面。

A: Thank you very much for coming.

B: 我们听说贵公司在中国市场非常有影响力，我们很想了解贵公司的业务情况和发展规划。

A: Thank you very much for your attention. We are dedicated to providing high-quality products and services, focusing on the research and development as well as sales in the chemical industry, and have achieved good performance in the Chinese market. Our development plan is to expand into the international market and we hope to cooperate with you.

B: 我们也非常有兴趣与贵公司合作。我们希望能够在技术方面与您合作，共同研发新产品。

A: We place a strong emphasis on technological innovation and R&D. Our skilled R&D team is well-equipped to collaborate with you on developing new products At the same time, we also focus on product quality and service, which can help you sell your products in the Chinese market.

B: 听起来不错。我们还希望了解贵公司的生产能力和工厂设备。

A: We have some advanced production equipment and lines to ensure the quality and efficiency of our products. If you'd like, we can give you a tour of our factory.

B: 非常感谢，我们很愿意了解您的生产设备和工厂。另外，贵公司的合作方式是怎样的呢？

A: Our cooperation approach is very flexible and we can develop suitable cooperation plans based on your needs and requirements. We can discuss specific details such as cooperation methods, time, and products. We attach great importance to mutual trust and win-win cooperation, and hope to establish a long-term and stable cooperative relationship with you.

B: 我们也非常赞同您这个合作理念。我们希望能够建立长期稳定的合作关系，并共同发展。

A: We are looking forward to establishing a cooperative relationship with you. If you have any questions or need further information, please feel free to contact us at any time.

B: 非常感谢，我们一定会的。

练习解析：

"We have heard that your company has a very influential position in the Chinese market."如译为"贵公司有非常有影响力的地位"显得非常累赘，"position（地位）"一词无须译出，直接译为"贵公司非常有影响力"即可。

"我们是一家致力于提供高品质产品和服务的公司，……"中的"公司"一词可减译，在上下文语境下，双方都理解是在讲中方企业。因此，可直接译为"我们致力于……"，即"We are dedicated to providing high-quality products and services …"

"We also strongly agree with the concept of mutual trust and win-win cooperation."由于前文已经提到了合作理念为"mutual trust and win-win cooperation"，因此此句可不必重复译出具体内容，即"我们也非常赞同您这个合作理念"。

Dialogue 3

原文：

A: 您好！我是美华镜业公司的出口部经理王鹏，这是我们的产品目录。

B: Thank you!

A: 目录上主要是我们2021年的产品系列。如果您对最新的产品感兴趣的话，我可以把今年最新的目录发邮件给您。

B: Thank you very much. I'd like to know which are the main export markets for your products?

A: 我公司的产品主要出口到北美、日本、欧盟等地区。美国是我们最大的出口目的地，去年出口美国的产品占到了总出口额的55%。

B: Your exhibits are very appealing, and the designs are truly unique. I believe there's a significant market for them in our country. Are you a manufacturer or a trading company?

A: 我们是一家生产商，在深圳和东莞都有自己的工厂，同时我公司也拥有进出口经营权，并且在香港设有办事处。

B: That sounds great! Do you have a product price list available?

A: 我们没有固定的价格表，如果您对哪个产品感兴趣，我可以提供给您一个参考价格。通常说，您订货的量越大，价格就会更优惠一些。

B: If I want to place an order, what is the minimum order quantity?

A: 5 000 件。

B: Where do you usually ship the goods from?

A: 香港，因为这样在成本上更加合理一些，而且在那有办事处。

B: I'm interested in the rectangular mirror model SH203 from your product catalog. Do you have any samples of it at the exhibition?

A: 非常遗憾，我们没有把这个型号带来展会。但是您可以去参观我们的工厂，这样可以对我们的产品有更详尽的了解。我们东莞的工厂离广州非常近，开车40分钟就可以到了。

B: I believe that's a great idea. However, I will be returning to my home country in three days. Is it possible to arrange the visit for tomorrow?

A: 没有问题。我会尽快安排，当一切安排好后我会电话通知您。

B: That's very kind of you. Thank you very much! See you tomorrow. Enjoy the day!

A: 谢谢！明天见！

参考译文：

A: Hello! I'm Wang Peng, the Export Manager at Meihua Mirror Company. Here is our product catalog.

B: 谢谢！

A: This catalog mainly showcases our 2021 product series. If you are interested in our latest products, I can send you this year's updated catalog via email.

B: 十分感谢，我想知道你们产品的主要出口市场是哪些？

A: Our company primarily exports products to North America, Japan, the European Union and other regions. The United States is our largest export destination, with products shipped there accounting for 55% of our total exports last year.

B: 你们的展品十分吸引人，设计也十分独特，相信在我们国家会大有市场。你们是生产商还是贸易公司？

A: We are a manufacturer with our own factories in both Shenzhen and Dongguan. Additionally, our company holds import and export rights, and we have an office in Hong Kong as well.

B: 听起来很不错啊。请问你们有没有产品价格表？

A: We don't operate with a fixed price list. If you're interested in a specific product, I can provide you with a reference price. Generally, the larger the order quantity, the more favorable the price will be.

B: 如果我想订货的话，最低的订货量是多少？

A: 5,000 pieces.

B: 在哪儿发货呢？

A: Hong Kong, because it's more cost-effective, and we also have an office there.

B: 我对产品目录里 SH203 型号的方镜很感兴趣，请问你们展会上有没有样品呢？

A: I'm sorry that the SH203 model isn't available at this exhibition. However, you are welcome to visit our factory, which would provide you with a more in-depth understanding of our products. Our factory in Dongguan is conveniently located, just a 40-minute drive from Guangzhou.

B: 这是个好主意。但是，我三天后就要回国了，不知可否安排在明天？

A: Of course. I will arrange it as soon as possible and give you a call once everything is set.

B: 真是太好了，非常感谢！明天见，祝您过得愉快！

A: Thanks! See you tomorrow!

练习解析：

本段原文需要基于语境对主语或宾语进行增译或减译。例如，"I believe there's a significant market for them in our country." 这一句的完整翻译为"我相信他们在我们国家会大有市场"，但由于上一句中 them 指代的展品作为主语，为了连接上一句并保持同一个主语，这句可省略主语 I 和宾语 them，即"相信在我们国家会大有市场"。此外，一些通用表达也可以通过增译或减译使译语表达更自然。例如，"I believe that's a great idea." 可减译为"这是个好主意"，而不用说"我相信这是个好主意"；"That's very nice of you." 可译为"真是太好了"，而不必加上主语译为"你真是太好了 / 你真好"，但这类表达更适用于关系较好的人之间。在翻译"Enjoy the day!"时则需加上表达祝福的词，可译为"祝您过得愉快 / 祝您度过愉快的一天"，而非"享受这一天"。

UNIT

第 6 单元

视译

视译是指看着源语稿时口头同步翻译出目的语，是同声传译中最常用的训练方法之一。译员的翻译速度如果和发言人的语速保持同步，这就是同声传译中的"带稿同传"，在大型国际商务会议和论坛等场合较常见。尽管本书主要关注对话口译，但视译练习也是口译学习者提升双语能力、提高目的语转换速度的重要形式。

6.1 视译准备步骤

译员在参加会议和论坛等活动时，一般会在活动前一天或当天拿到演讲稿。译员可以采取以下六个小步骤，充分做好译前准备。

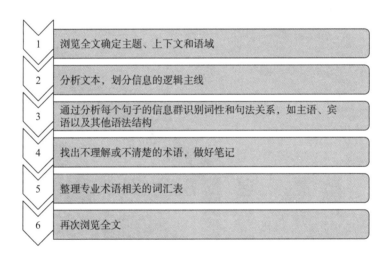

1	浏览全文确定主题、上下文和语域
2	分析文本，划分信息的逻辑主线
3	通过分析每个句子的信息群识别词性和句法关系，如主语、宾语以及其他语法结构
4	找出不理解或不清楚的术语，做好笔记
5	整理专业术语相关的词汇表
6	再次浏览全文

6.2 视译原则

视译遵循两大原则：断句和顺句驱动，同时适当进行增补。断句是指将英语或汉语首先根据意群进行划分，再分别译成目的语。在拿到原文文稿时，可以边看边用斜线（/）划分意群。顺句驱动是在划分意群的基础上，不对译文进行大范围的语序调整，自然地把各个语句串联起来。如果不调整语序就很难译顺，可以提前在文稿上做好调整顺序的标记（如箭头、增添号等）。

除此之外，可在文稿适当地方做上其他所需记号，你需要在练习中找到适合自己的记录习惯。

句子精练

请在以下句子的适当地方做上视译所需记号，并进行视译。

1. So let's move straight into the main purpose of today's presentation.

2. The global community is redefining what success means by challenging the traditional routes taken to get there.

3. A renewed focus on work life balance is becoming increasingly important, especially in parenting.

4. 目前正在推动社会全面进步，号召社会接受能力、性别、文化背景的不同。

5. T 台服装样式增加，虽然这意味着我们朝着正确的方向迈进，但还不够。

6. 自由职业者文化的灵活性和自主权有助于他们享受浪漫的慢生活。

6.3 视译练习技巧

除了译前准备，译员平时也可以从以下五个方面提升视译技巧和翻译水平。

6.3.1 阅读理解及视译

选择一篇带参考译文的演讲稿，中文或英文皆可。首先，通读全文，确保理解文章的主要内容和要点，然后将其视译成目的语，尽量保持准确和流畅的表达。可以把自己练习视译的过程进行录音并转写，一字一句，即包括停顿、重复等都记录下来，以便准确发现自己口译中出现的问题。

6.3.2　双语对比

对比自己的视译版本和原始翻译之间的差异，分析并理解其中的不同之处。这个方法可以帮助发现自己在双语表达上的问题并进行合适的翻译选择。原始翻译由于可能是笔译，在翻译语序上可能更符合目的语的表达习惯，但不一定适用于视译过程。在对比过程中，学习者应着重思考如何调整表达，以更符合视译的顺句驱动原则。

6.3.3　反向翻译

练习时，将讲稿的参考译文反向翻译为源语。这个过程可以帮助学习者锻炼双语转化能力，提高语言表达的敏感性和准确度，同时也是对前两步练习过程的复习和巩固。

6.3.4　同声传译

如讲稿配有录音，建议先尝试段落口译。初始阶段，可选择一小段内容听录音后进行目的语的视译，随后再继续听下一部分。经一定训练后，可试行边听边实时翻译，即进入同声传译阶段。此方法有助于磨炼同步听取与翻译的能力，进而提高反应迅速性与口头表达。但必须关注与发言者间的时间差，尽量缩短时间差以获得更多内容，确保翻译丰富完整。重要的是，同声传译绝不能影响发言的时效性。

6.3.5　模拟练习

与同伴组成小组进行模拟练习，可以选择模拟商务对话、会议或其他日常场景，讲者需提前准备好讲稿并给到译员。在模拟练习时，译员尝试进行即时视译。这样可以帮助提高在真实交流中的翻译技能和语言应对能力。译员和讲者可以互换角色进行练习。

以上方法可以帮助口译初学者在中英双语练习视译时进行有效的练习和提高。持续的练习和积累经验才是提高视译能力的关键。

6.4 口译练习

练习1

Text 1

请用 5 分钟通读以下演讲稿,理解原文大意,在适当地方标记出断句、顺序调整及其他所需记号,并将文章视译出来。第二遍练习可根据能力水平,尝试边听录音边视译。

词汇预习

海伦司	Helen's
行业媒体	industry media
后疫情时代	post-pandemic era
营销政策	marketing policy

原文:

尊敬的各位嘉宾,亲爱的合作伙伴们!大家晚上好!

今天,我们又迎来了海伦司一年一度的交流会,在座的各位与我们海伦司公司一路相互扶持,共同走来。

多年来,我们彼此信任,结下了深厚的情谊,在此我也代表公司欢迎各位在百忙之中抽空参加本次大会,欢迎各位朋友的到来!

出席本次会议的还有公司的主要领导和行业媒体的朋友们,在此,也欢迎大家的到来!

今年,我们取得了不错的销售成绩,也在中国开阔了更大的市场。但同时我们也应该清醒地认识到存在的问题。在后疫情时代,只有我们共同努力才能战胜一切困难!

公司的事业也是在座各位的事业，希望大家听完2023年营销政策和市场规划后，会对来年的工作充满信心。

相信在新的一年里我们携手共进，再创佳绩，再铸辉煌！谢谢大家。

Text 2

本文为深圳技术大学阮双琛校长在2022年11月深圳技术大学与波恩莱茵锡格应用技术大学国际跨学科线上系列讲座"工程学与新创精神"开幕式上的致辞。请用10分钟通读以下演讲稿，理解原文大意，在适当地方标记出断句、顺序调整及其他所需记号，并将文章视译出来。第二遍练习可根据能力水平，尝试边听录音边视译。

词汇预习

- "工程学与新创精神"国际跨学科线上系列讲座
  International Interdisciplianry Digital Lecture Series "Engineering and Entrepreneurship"
- 先进学科和项目
  advanced disciplines and programs
- 波恩莱茵锡格应用技术大学
  Bonn-Rhein-Sieg University of Applied Sciences (H-BRS)
- 先进教学方法合作研讨会
  Collaborative Workshop on Advanced Teaching Methods
- "互联世界中的可持续发展与创新"国际跨学科线上系列讲座
  International Interdisciplinary Virtual Lecture Series "Sustainability and Innovation in Connected World"

原文：

Distinguished Vice President Jürgen Bode,

Dear Prof. Franz Raps,

Ladies and gentlemen,

Good afternoon!

On behalf of Shenzhen Technology University, I am greatly honored to be with you today to witness the opening ceremony of the 2nd International Interdisciplianry Digital Lecture Series "Engineering and Entrepreneurship". Please allow me to take this opportunity to convey my gratitude to our important international partner Bonn-Rhein-Sieg University of Applied Sciences (H-BRS), and the colleagues from SZTU for their great support and efforts to make this event possible! Especially, I would like to thank Vice President Bode and Prof. Raps who made great efforts to mobilize all online resources and build a learning platform for both Chinese and German students.

With the strong support from Guangdong Province, Shenzhen City and our international partners, Shenzhen Technology University has emerged as a high-level and international university of applied sciences and technology since its establishment in 2016. Over the past six years, SZTU spares no effort in strengthening the international cooperation with our partners, accelerating the infrastructure development and creating sound learning environment for our students. It's worth mentioning that SZTU has broken a new record in student enrollment. This September, we welcomed about 4,000 freshmen. With rapid campus construction, we are confident that we can accommodate more students and march into a new chapter.

We aim to set up advanced disciplines and programs by cooperating with international partners. So far, we have signed MoUs with 68 overseas universities, institutions and enterprises from 17 countries and regions. Our international cooperation achievements include joint laboratories, offices, student exchange programs and online workshops or courses during the COVID-19 Pandemic. Before the Pandemic, we organized International Week every year and attracted many international professors, partners and students.

The friendship between our two universities began when Vice President Bode visited SZTU in April and November 2019. In January, 2020, SZTU delegation visited H-BRS for the first time, our two universities signed a cooperation agreement to strengthen cooperation in teacher-student exchange programs and training projects. Since then, our two universities have been committed to launching learning programs. In June 2021, we organized the successful Collaborative Workshop on Advanced Teaching Methods, the teachers from both universities shared their teaching experience to improve teaching ability. In October 2021, the first International Interdisciplinary Virtual Lecture Series "Sustainability and Innovation in Connected World" was launched and achieved a great success. Both German and Chinese students have gained a lot from those online lectures.

Today I'm very happy to see the 2nd International Digital Lecture Series "Engineering and Entrepreneurship" is officially launched. I am confident that it will be another successful cooperative program. Through this program, we not only expect our students to gain professional knowledge in engineering technology and entrepreneurship, but also to improve their cross-cultural communication skills.

Although the COVID-19 pandemic has suspended many international exchange programs, we are optimistic that we will find out new ways to increase international cooperation in launching exchange programs, lectures and courses in the future. To provide better campus environment for international students, our Apartment Complex for International Teachers and Students, Smart Classrooms and modern canteens increase our confidence to host international students. In the future, we are ready to welcome international students with our well-equipped facilities and campus environment.

Finally, I'd like to extend my thanks to all the teachers of this lecture series. And I wish this seminar a great success. Thank you very much!

练习2

Dialogue 1

四人小组对话口译练习，两人为讲者，两人为译员。当然，你也可以通过扫码进行自主练习，在提示音后进行口译。

词汇预习

促进排便	promote bowel movements
纯天然的	pure natural
加拿大卫生部	Health Canada
运费优惠	freight discount

Dialogue 2

四人组成小组进行对话口译练习,可互换讲者和译员角色。同样,你也可以进行自主练习。

词汇预习

化妆品	cosmetics
成分	ingredient
国家药品监督管理局	the National Medical Products Administration (NMPA)
指示性的	indicative
付款交单	Documents against Payment (D/P)
承兑交单	Documents against Acceptance (D/A)
不可撤销	irrevocable
装运单据	shipping document
信用证	Letter of Credit (L/C)
运费	freight

Dialogue 3

请预习词汇,并用 5 分钟通读对话,理解原文大意,在适当地方标记出断句、顺序调整及其他所需记号,边听录音边视译。

词汇预习

应用技术大学	university of applied sciences
国际合作与学生工作部	International Cooperation and Student Affairs Office
东巴伐利亚应用技术大学（雷根斯堡）	OTH Regensburg
联合培养模式	joint education models
国际周授课	lectures at International Week
工匠精神	spirit of craftsmanship
学生交换项目	student exchange program

原文：

A: 您好，我是深圳技术大学国际合作与学生工作部的 Loran。

B: Welcome to OTH Regensburg. I'm Rachel from the international office.

A: 深圳技术大学是一所高标准建设的国际化、高水平、示范性应用技术大学。一直以来，我们坚持培养更多具有国际视野、工匠精神的研究技术型人才。通过这一次的访问，我们真诚希望与贵校能够继续加强学术交流与合作，共同培养更多的技术型、创新型人才。

B: OTH Regensburg is a renowned public university in Germany and one of the largest universities of applied sciences in Bavaria. We are well-known for our high-quality teaching and outstanding applied research. It seems that we have a shared focus on talent development. Our strengths in technology and disciplines complement each other well, which can lead to mutually beneficial collaboration between our two universities.

A: 的确，在我们现有的合作交流成果上，我们可以进一步拓展合作领域与合作方式，推动两校在联合培养模式、国际周授课等方面取得新突破。

B: Additionally, we can explore more student exchange opportunities, allowing students to study and live at each other's universities. This will give them insights into different cultures and educational systems, further strengthening our collaboration.

A: 确实，毕竟现在疫情放开了，我们也非常希望能够拥有更多的机会与贵校进行更深入的学术交流。

B: We can further discuss the details of the student exchange program in our future collaborations. Thank you for your visit.

6.5 练习原文、译文及解析

句子精练

1. **原文：** So let's move straight into the main purpose / of today's presentation.

   参考译文： 所以让我们直奔主题，聊聊今天的内容。

2. **原文：** The global community is redefining / what success means / by challenging the traditional routes taken / to get there.

   参考译文： 国际社会正在重新定义成功，挑战传统意义上成功的方式。

3. **原文：** A renewed focus on work life balance / is becoming increasingly important, / especially in parenting.

   参考译文： 重新关注工作与生活平衡变得日益重要，尤其是在养育子女方面。

4. **原文：** 目前正在推动社会全面进步 /，号召社会接受 /ˬ 能力、性别、文化背景的（不同）。

   参考译文： There's a push for more progressive societies to embrace the differences in ability, gender, cultural background.

5. **原文：** T 台服装样式的增加 /，虽然意味着我们朝着正确的方向迈进，但这还不够。

参考译文： There are increasing diversity of all kinds on the runways. Although it is a step in the right direction, it's not enough on its own.

6. **原文：** 自由职业者文化特有的灵活性 / 和自主权 / 有助于享受浪漫的慢生活。

参考译文： Freelance culture featuring flexibility and the idea of access over ownership contributes to the romance of a slow pace of life.

练习 1

Text 1

参考译文：

Distinguished guests, dear partners, good evening!

Today, we gather here at the Helens' annual exchange meeting. Everyone presents here and Helen's, have supported each other along the way.

Over the years, we have trusted each other and developed deep friendship. I, on behalf of the company, welcome all of you who take time out of your busy schedule to participate in this conference. Thank you to be with us.

We are also joined by the main leaders of the company and friends from the industry media. I would also want to extend warm welcome to you!

We have achieved good sales and expanded the market in China. However, we should also be aware of the existing problems. In the post-pandemic era, only by working together can we overcome all difficulties.

The cause of the company is also the cause of everyone present here. After listening to the 2023 marketing policy and plan, I hope that everyone will have full confidence in the work of next year.

I believe that in the new year, we can work together to create new achievements and create a brilliant future! Thank you.

练习解析：

视译前的阅读环节，应将专有名词（如"海伦司"）和不懂的词汇标注在文中。同时，按断句和顺句驱动原则在文中划斜线（/）。如果需要调整语序或改变词性以顺应原文顺序，可在对应位置适当标注一些词。例如，“在座的各位与我们海伦司公司一路相互扶持，共同走来”中的“共同走来”，不适合直译为“walk together”，原文意思应为“一路上”互相扶持，直接补充“along the way”以符合英文语境。

图 6–1 展示了一名译员如何在稿子上做标记以方便视译。当然，这与交传的口译笔记法一样，具有个人风格，同学们应在练习过程中形成自己的标记习惯。

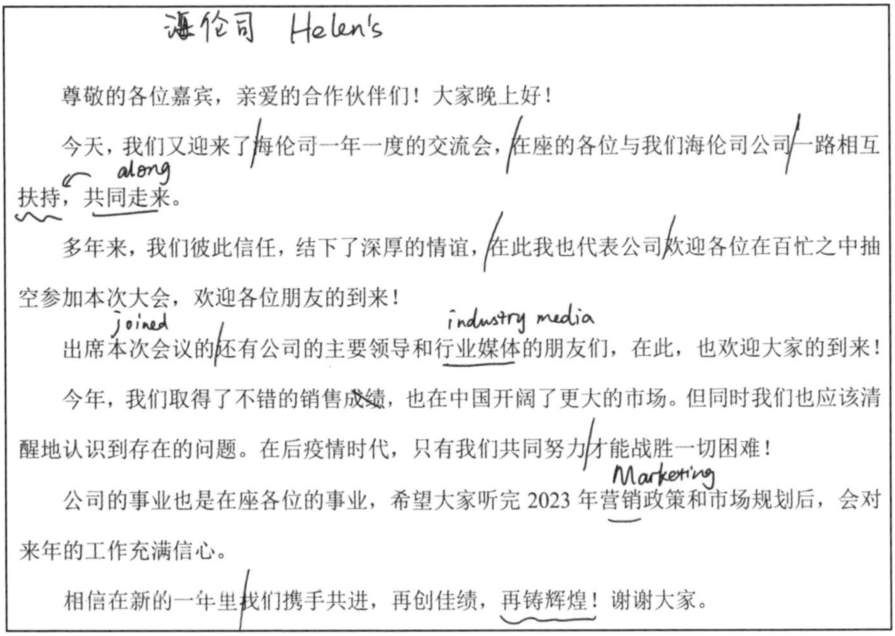
海伦司 Helen's

尊敬的各位嘉宾，亲爱的合作伙伴们！大家晚上好！

今天，我们又迎来了海伦司一年一度的交流会，在座的各位与我们海伦司公司一路相互扶持，共同走来。

多年来，我们彼此信任，结下了深厚的情谊，在此我也代表公司欢迎各位在百忙之中抽空参加本次大会，欢迎各位朋友的到来！

出席本次会议的还有公司的主要领导和行业媒体的朋友们，在此，也欢迎大家的到来！

今年，我们取得了不错的销售成绩，也在中国开阔了更大的市场。但同时我们也应该清醒地认识到存在的问题。在后疫情时代，只有我们共同努力才能战胜一切困难！

公司的事业也是在座各位的事业，希望大家听完 2023 年营销政策和市场规划后，会对来年的工作充满信心。

相信在新的一年里我们携手共进，再创佳绩，再铸辉煌！谢谢大家。

图 6–1　视译标记（1）

Text 2

参考译文:

尊敬的 Jürgen Bode 副校长，

尊敬的 Franz Raps 教授，

女士们，先生们，

下午好！

我代表深圳技术大学，非常荣幸与大家在今天共同见证第二期"工程学与新创精神"国际跨学科线上系列讲座开幕式。请允许我借此机会表达我的谢意，感谢我们的重要国际合作伙伴波恩—莱茵—锡格应用技术大学和深圳技术大学的同事们，感谢他们的大力支持和努力，使此次活动顺利举行！我要特别感谢 Bode 副校长和 Raps 教授，他们付出了巨大努力，调动所有线上资源，搭建了一个学习平台提供给中德学生。

在广东省、深圳市和各国际合作伙伴的大力支持下，深圳技术大学自 2016 年成立以来，致力于成为一所高水平、国际化的应用技术大学。六年来，深技大不遗余力地加强与合作伙伴的国际合作，加快基础设施建设，为学生创造良好的学习环境。值得一提的是，深圳技术大学在招生方面打破了新纪录。今年 9 月，我们迎来了大约 4 000 名新生。随着校园建设的快速推进，我们有信心容纳更多的学生，迈向新的篇章。

我们致力于通过与国际合作伙伴的合作，建立先进的学科和项目。到目前为止，我们已经与来自 17 个国家和地区的 68 所海外大学、机构和企业签署了合作备忘录。我们的国际合作成果包括联合实验室及办公室、学生交流交换项目和在线研讨会或课程，这些都发生在新冠肺炎大流行期间。在疫情暴发之前，我们每年都组织国际周，吸引了许多国际教授、合作伙伴和学生前来参与。

我们两校间的友谊始于 Bode 副校长访问深圳技术大学，那是在 2019 年 4 月和 11 月。2020 年 1 月，深圳技术大学代表团首次访问波恩莱茵锡格应用技术大学，双方签署合作协议，加强师生交流项目和培训项目的合作。从那时起，我们的两所大学一直致力于推动学习项目。2021 年 6 月，我们成功举办了"先进教学方法合作研讨会"，两校教师分享了他们的教学经验，提高教学能力。2021 年 10 月，首届国际跨学科线上系列讲座"互联世界中的可持续发展与创新"启动并取得了巨大成功，中德两国的学生都从这些在线讲座中收获颇丰。

今天，我非常高兴地看到第二期"工程学与新创精神"国际跨学科线上系列讲座正式启动。我相信这将是另一个成功的合作项目。通过这个项目，我们不仅希望我们的学生获得工程技术和创业方面的专业知识，还希望提高他们的跨文化沟通技能。

尽管新冠疫情中断了许多国际交流项目，但我们很高兴将找到新途径加强国际合作，比如在开展交流项目、讲座和课程方面。为了提供更好的校园环境给国际学生，我们的外籍教师与留学生综合楼、智能教室和现代化的食堂增强了我们接待国际学生的信心。在未来，我们已经做好充分准备，欢迎国际学生的到来，我们有着完善的设备设施和校园环境。

最后，我要感谢参与本次系列讲座的各位老师。祝愿这次研讨会取得圆满成功。感谢大家！

练习解析：

由于英文中时间、地点、介词短语等会放置于句末，英译汉时往往需要适当调整语序。如按顺句驱动原则无法符合语言表达习惯时，可在稿子中提前标注，如将增添号（∧）、中括号、画线等表示要将句子靠后的内容提前到插入符号处。如图 6-2，该段落中将"通过与国际伙伴合作"这一信息移到前面，使句子表达更顺畅；将"来自 17 个国家和地区"移到"68 个海外高校"之前，更符合中文表达习惯，并标注上"17"以提醒翻译时要插入后方内容。

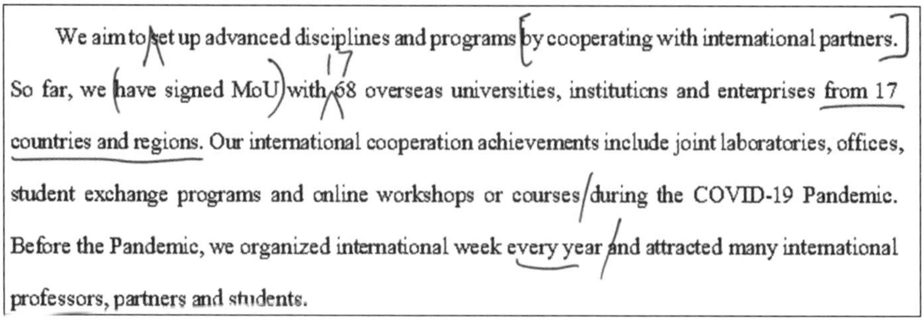

> We aim to [set up advanced disciplines and programs] by cooperating with international partners.]
> So far, we have signed MoU with ∧17 68 overseas universities, institutions and enterprises from 17 countries and regions. Our international cooperation achievements include joint laboratories, offices, student exchange programs and online workshops or courses / during the COVID-19 Pandemic. Before the Pandemic, we organized international week every year / and attracted many international professors, partners and students.

图 6-2 视译标记（2）

练习 2

Dialogue 1

原文：

A: 您好，我是来自深圳的采购专员 Eddy，很高兴能够与您见面。

B: Welcome to Canada. I'm, Dr. Daily's Marketing Manager Jason. Please take a seat!

A: 我们对贵公司研制的纯天然促进排便的粉剂很感兴趣，您可以介绍一下该产品的详细情况吗？

B: Thank you very much for your interest in our product. Our product is mainly made of natural plant extracts, which can effectively promote bowel movements and relieve constipation. Our product has passed strict certification by Health Canada and meets the highest safety and quality standards.

A: 我们还想要了解一些关于产品价格和配送方式的信息。

B: Our product price is 20 Canadian dollars per bottle, with 300 grams of powder per bottle. We can ship the product by sea or air, and the specific cost will depend on the order quantity and shipping distance.

A: 我们计划可以订购 10 000 瓶，空运到深圳，不知道是否有什么优惠吗？

B: If you can order 15,000 bottles or more at once, we can offer you a discounted price of 18 Canadian dollars per bottle.

A: 这个优惠非常吸引人，但考虑到我们的库存和市场需求，一次性订购过多的产品风险比较大。如果您能够提供一些运费优惠，我们可能会考虑增加订购量。

B: We understand your need, but the cost of transportation is also an important consideration for us. The specific freight discount scheme is subject to the exact order quantity and delivery time that you finally provide.

A: 好的，我们会再仔细考虑，另外，我们还需要了解一下贵公司接受的付款方式和大约的交货期。

B: We accept payment by wire transfer and letter of credit. The delivery time is approximately 7～10 working days, and the specific time will also depend on the shipping method and location.

A: 请问贵公司是否可以提供样品，以便我们进行测试和评估？

B: Of course, we can provide free samples, and you only need to pay the shipping cost.

A: 好的，非常感谢贵公司的支持，我们会尽快对产品进行测试和评估。

B: We hope for a successful partnership.

参考译文:

A: Hello, I am Eddy, a sourcing specialist from Shenzhen. So glad to meet you.

B: 欢迎来到加拿大，我是 Dr. Daily 的市场部经理 Jason，请坐！

A: We are very interested in the pure natural powder that promotes bowel movements developed by your company. Could you give us some details about the product?

B: 非常感谢您对我们产品的关注。我们的产品主要是由天然植物提取物制成，可以有效促进排便，缓解便秘问题。我们的产品通过了加拿大卫生部的严格认证，符合最高的安全和质量标准。

A: We also would like to inquire about the price and shipping methods.

B: 我们的产品价格是每瓶 20 加元，每瓶含有 300 克的粉末。配送方式我们可以通过海运或者航空运输，具体费用需要根据订单量和运输距离来计算。

A: We plan to order 10,000 bottles by air to Shenzhen. Is there any discount available?

B: 如果您能够一次性订购 15 000 瓶以上的话，我们可以为您提供优惠价格，每瓶的价格可以降至 18 加元。

A: This offer is very attractive. But given the stock and market demand, it is risky to order too much at one time. If you are able to offer some shipping discounts, we may consider increasing the order quantity.

B: 我们理解您的需求，不过运输成本对我们来说也是很重要的考虑因素。具体的运费优惠方案还需根据您方最终提供的确切订单量和交货时间而定。

A: Okay, we will think about it more carefully. Also, we need to know about the payment method and the approximate delivery date.

B: 我们接受电汇和信用证的付款方式。交货时间大概需要 7～10 个工作日，具体时间也需要根据运输方式和地点而定。

A: Would you be willing to provide samples for us to test and evaluate?

B: 当然可以，我们可以免费提供样品，您只需要支付运输费用即可。

A: We appreciate your support so much. We will test and evaluate the product as soon as possible.

B: 合作愉快。

练习解析：

本对话涉及一些专有名词，如"Health Canada"，应在预习词汇环节提前想好对应笔记符号，如 HC，在口译过程中可以快速记录并译出。

对话中还有不少数字，应特别注意数字后所带单位或量词，如"Canadian dollars""gram"等，笔记中应记好"C$""g"等，避免出现数字对了但单位错了的情况。

Dialogue 2

原文：

A: Good afternoon. Nice to meet you! My name is Zoe. I am the sales representative of Z Overseas Cosmetics Import and Export Company.

B: 很高兴有机会能够拜访贵公司，我是王氏化妆品企业的采购经理。

A: Welcome! What is the main topic of this visit?

B: 我们需要购进一批口红作为我们旗下门店新季度的上新产品，希望您能为我详细地介绍一下。

A: I'm glad to provide you with all the information you need. These products are competitively positioned in the high-end cosmetics market and have gained popularity. Would you like to have a look?

B: 好的，都有哪些样式呢？并且我想知道这些产品的成分是否安全，是否符合我国国家药品监督管理局的法规要求。

A: We have many selections. Please refer to Page 8 of this manual for an introduction. At the same time, you can check page 16 for the comparison table of product ingredients.

B: 我了解了，可以提供一个平均指示性单价吗？

A: All right. Take this one, for example. The unit price is 250 RMB.

B: 大量购买的话你们提供折扣吗？

A: Yes, usually about 20%, but it depends on the quantity ordered.

B: 可以考虑，您方接受付款交单或承兑交单吗？

A: I'm afraid not. We only accept payment by irrevocable letter of credit against shipping documents.

B: 您知道如此大金额的信用证对您来说没有影响，但对我们影响很大。

A: Actually, it affects us too.

B: 如果您在本月前发货的话，我们将同意。

A: All right.

B: 并且我想了解一下你们的运输方式。

A: Sea transportation, and we bear the freight.

B: 好的，我们订购这三款产品的这些款式各 8000 支。

A: OK. Shall we sign the contract now?

B: 好的，没有问题。非常感谢，希望合同执行过程一切顺利！

参考译文：

A: 下午好，很高兴见到你们！我叫 Zoe，是 Z 海外化妆品进出口公司的销售代表。

B: I'm glad to have the opportunity to visit your company. I'm the purchasing manager of Wang's Cosmetics Enterprise.

A: 欢迎你们的到来！这次来访主要想商讨什么呢？

B: We need to buy a batch of lipsticks as the new products of our stores in the new season. I hope you can tell me more about them.

A: 我非常乐意地提供您所需要的一切信息。我们这几款产品品牌在化妆品高端市场都有一定的市场竞争力与知名度，不知道您是否想看一看？

B: Ok, what kind of products do you have? And I want to know whether the ingredients of these products are safe and comply with the regulations of the National Medical Products Administration.

A: 我们有很多的款式可供选择，您看一下这份手册的第 8 页，其中有对应介绍。同时，您可以查看手册第 16 页关于产品成分的对照表。

B: I see. Could you give me an average indicative unit price?

A: 比如这款，它的单价为 250 元人民币。

B: Do you offer discounts for large quantities?

A: 是的，通常是 20% 左右，但要根据订货量来定。

B: May I consider it. Do you accept D/P or D/A?

A: 恐怕不行，我们只接受不可撤销的信用证，凭装运单据付款。

B: You know an L/C for such a large amount means nothing to you but a lot to us.

A: 事实上对我们也有影响。

B: We'll agree if you deliver the goods before this month.

A: 好吧。

B: And I'd like to know your mode of transportation.

A: 海运，并且我们承担运费。

B: OK. We order 8000 pieces of each of these three products.

A: 好的，那么我们这就签订合同，可以吗？

B: OK, no problem. Thank you very much. I hope everything goes well with the contract implementation!

练习解析：

本对话有不少商务专业词汇，如付款交单、承兑交单、不可撤销的信用证等。通过平常的练习，要积累相关词汇双语表达，形成长期记忆。

Dialogue 3

参考译文：

A: Hello. I am Loran from International Cooperation and Student Affairs Office at Shenzhen Technology University.

B: 欢迎来到东巴伐利亚应用技术大学（雷根斯堡）。我是 Rachel，来自国际部。

A: Shenzhen Technology University is an international, high-level, and exemplary university of applied sciences. We have consistently been committed to nurturing research-oriented technical talents with international perspectives and a spirit of craftsmanship. Through this visit, we sincerely hope to join hands with your university to further enhance academic exchanges and cooperation, fostering more technically proficient and innovative talents together.

B: 东巴伐利亚应用技术大学（雷根斯堡）是一所著名的德国公立大学，也是巴伐利亚州最大的应用技术大学之一。众所周知，我校拥有高质量的教学和卓越的应用研究水平。由此看来，我们双方有一定共识，体现在人才培养方面，而且我们的优势在技术和学科方面可以互补，这一切可促成双方的互利合作。

A: Indeed, building upon the existing collaborative achievements, we can further expand cooperation areas and methods. This can promote our cooperation in joint education models, lectures at International Week, and other areas to achieve breakthroughs.

B: 除此之外，我们可以开展更多学生交换项目，让学生到对方学校学习和生活，这样可以使他们了解不同的文化和教育体系，同时加强我们双方的合作。

A: Certainly, especially now that the situation with the pandemic has improved, we are very eager to seize more opportunities for in-depth academic exchanges with your university.

B: 我们可以在后续合作中进一步探讨交换生项目的详情事宜。感谢您的来访。

练习解析：

　　此段对话大多可顺译，但部分语句需调整语序，按中文表达习惯来翻译。在视译时，需要通过意群划分、适当断句、增译减译和词性转换，以实现顺句驱动，同时确保表达通畅。比如"We are well-known for our..."可译为"众所周知，我校拥有……"；"we share common ground / in talent development, and our strengths / in technology and disciplines / complement each other"可顺译为"我们双方有一定共识，体现在人才培养方面，而且我们的优势在技术和学科方面可以互补"；"我们真诚希望与贵校能够……"这一句可顺译为"we sincerely hope to join hands with your university to..."；"推动两校在……等方面取得新突破"可独立为一句，顺译为"This can promote our cooperation in... and other areas to achieve breakthroughs"。

UNIT 7

第 7 单元

直译与意译

第 6 单元介绍了增译和减译这两个常用的口译技巧，本单元介绍直译和意译这两种最基本的翻译方法，囊括增译、减译等多个技巧，且两者相辅相成、互为补充。

7.1 直译与意译

7.1.1 直译与意译的区别

直译就是既保持源语内容又保持源语形式，要求目的语与源语在用词、句法结构、比喻及风格特征等方面尽可能趋同。意译则是只保持源语内容不保持源语句法和语法形式，重在传递信息，使译文在用词、句法结构、风格特征等方面尽可能贴近目的语表达习惯，便于听者理解[1]。通过以下例句可直观了解两者的区别：

原文：时间就像沙漏，无论你怎么逃避，它总会流逝。

直译：Time is like an hourglass. No matter how you escape, it will always pass.

意译：Time flies like sand through the hourglass, it slips away no matter how you resist.

直译保留了源语的语序、结构和词汇的字面意义；而意译通过增补、改变词汇和调换语序，按目的语表达习惯更自然地传达了源语意思。原句中"逃避"意译为"resist"，即"无论你怎么阻挡"，更自然地衔接了"时间像沙漏总会流逝"这一比喻。

7.1.2 直译与意译的选择

商务对话通常用词专业严谨、简洁易懂、语言规范、内容具体明确，多数情况下直译能准确传递源语的完整内容，保留语体风格。然而，商务对话也存在精炼、委婉等特点，由于英语和汉语在句式结构、语法和社会文化背景等方面都有所差异，意译才能准确传递信息。

此外，由于商务对话口译具有即时性，且商务场合时有时需无笔记交替传译，

---

[1] 朱林韬. 2010. 浅析商务英语中的直译与意译. 中外教育研究,（9）: 3.

译员难以逐字完整记忆，也不能长时间字字斟酌推敲，要以精练的目的语准确传达讲者的原意，让听者迅速理解，达到跨文化交际目的。这就意味着口译不宜逐字直译或生搬硬套地字面翻译，也要避免不着边际的意译或过度翻译，应根据实际情况灵活地结合直译和意译，选择效果更佳的译法，迅速产出准确的表达，以确保口译更贴近原意并符合听众的语言习惯。

7.2 直译的运用

为确保短时间内及时精准地翻译，口译尤其是同声传译，通常会遵循顺句驱动原则，即根据源语的顺序来翻译，把长句按照意群来断句，再用连接词把意群串联起来。译员在顺句驱动原则下应优先使用直译法。尤其当源语的句子结构、逻辑顺序与目的语较为接近时，直译能使目的语表达通顺自然。

商务对话中，涉及公司介绍、产品信息、数量、质量、价格、订单需求等客观信息类文本以及专业术语时，应运用直译法，以确保信息的精准传递。商务谈判等场合涉及情绪或情感的表达时，也应尽量采取直译法，以准确传达讲者的态度和目的。

但口译中直译不等于死译硬译，而是要灵活按源语的逻辑关系对信息进行拆分或整合，有时需要进行增译或减译来衔接语句的前后逻辑。此外，许多英语词汇已通过直译广泛应用于汉语中，中英两种语言中也存在许多文化相通、含义广为流传的短语和习语等，翻译这些表达时采用直译会更加生动形象，如以下示例：

- hot line 热线
- pillar industry 支柱产业
- chain reaction 连锁反应
- A rising tide lifts all boats. 水涨众船高。
- 黑市 black market
- 绿色食品 green food
- 沉默是金 Silence is golden.
- 血浓于水 Blood is thicker than water.

练习 1

请听录音,逐句进行口译。

7.3 意译的运用

在商务对话交传中,若讲者单次讲话时间长、信息量大,译员难以完整直译出讲者的完整话语时,可采取意译法,即"得意忘形",这意味着脱离源语语言的外在形式,不拘泥于字词,而是领会整段话的意思并有所取舍,重在传递主要信息。

考虑到中英文化差异,译员有时按源语的字面意义和语序直译,可能无法准确表达源语的文化内涵或讲者传递的信息,导致目的语语法或逻辑不通,甚至引起曲解。这时就需要采用意译法,通过变通源语语序、语法、词汇或修辞手法,或进行解释性翻译,来传达源语的真正含义。例如,将"拳头产品"直译为"fist product"显然不对,可按实际意思译为"the most competitive product";"干货"若直译为"dry goods",在英式英语中是指米面、咖啡、茶叶等干货,而美式英语中则是指纺织品,容易产生歧义[1]。因此应根据实际语境进行意译,若指食品中的"干货"可译为"dried food",若指内容的干货可译为 practical information。

尤其是针对包含典故或文化不相通的词句,或不符合目的语习惯表达的内容,应结合语境,按照目的语习惯和文化背景进行意译。例如"鹬蚌相争,渔翁得利",应进行解释性翻译,传达其寓意:"The third party benefits when two parties fight each other."

以下是部分短语的意译示例[2]:

- a land of honey and milk 鱼米之乡
- keep something under one's hat 保密

---

1 朱林韬. 2010. 浅析商务英语中的直译与意译. 中外教育研究,(9): 3.

2 冯庆华. 1997. 实用翻译教程英汉互译. 上海:上海外语教育出版社.

- look before you leap 三思而后行
- 大刀阔斧 in a bold and resolute way
- 拦路虎 a lion in the way/obstacles
- 开门见山 come straight to the point

练习 2

请听录音，逐句进行口译。

7.4 口译练习

练习 1

Text 1

请听录音，这是一段关于探讨中国商务文化的演讲。请先预习词汇，口译时尝试使用本单元学到的直译和意译方法。录音已分割为多个语段，请在提示音后暂停录音并开始口译。

词汇预习

文化价值观	cultural values
基石	bedrock
人际关系	interpersonal relationships
谦虚	humility

Text 2

请听录音，这是一段关于探讨全球商业背景下跨文化交流的讲话。请先预习词汇，口译时尝试使用本单元学到的直译和意译方法。录音已分割为多个语段，请在提示音后暂停录音并开始口译。

词汇预习

细微差别	nuances
权力差距	power distance
个人主义	individualism
集体主义	collectivism
不确定性规避	uncertainty avoidance
高语境的沟通风格	high-context communication style
融洽	rapport
文化内涵	cultural connotations

练习 2

Dialogue 1

四人小组对话口译练习,两人为讲者,两人为译员。当然,你也可以通过扫码进行自主练习,在提示音后进行口译。

词汇预习

实木地板	solid wood flooring
人力	manpower
海运	sea freight
分批装运	partial shipment
装船	ship the goods
一式两份	in duplicate

Dialogue 2

四人小组对话口译练习,可互换讲者和译员角色。同样,你也可以进行自主练习。

词汇预习

调查	investigate
品牌知名度	brand awareness
广告宣传活动	advertising campaign
酒香不怕巷子深。	Good wine needs no bush.

Dialogue 3

四人小组对话口译练习，自选讲者和译员角色。同样，你也可以进行自主练习。

词汇预习

捆绑销售	bundled sales
跨领域合作	cross-domain collaboration
联名产品	co-branded product
市场反响	market response

7.5　练习原文、译文及解析

练习1

1. **原文**: My boss once said a word that remains engraved on my mind. He said, "Stop seeing anything in black and white. Try to take another way to look at an issue."

   参考译文: 我上司曾说过一句话，一直铭刻在我脑海里。他说："不要看什么

151

事都非黑即白，试着换个方式看问题。"

解析：这句话的结构与中文表达习惯相通，可按源语语序直译，并根据意群断句，第一句即分为"My boss once said a word"和"(the word) remains engraved on my mind"这两个意群。其中"engraved on my mind"直译为"铭刻在我脑海里"可还原源语的修辞手法。此外，"see... in black and white"是指用非对即错、简单绝对的眼光看问题，在中文中有相通的表述，即"非黑即白"。因此可以直译为"非黑即白"，更加还原原话。

2. **原文**：在春节期间，家家户户都会贴春联，张贴福字，共同庆祝这个传统的节日。

参考译文：During the Spring Festival, every household will paste Spring Festival couplets and hang up the Chinese character "fu", which means blessing, to celebrate this traditional holiday.

解析：这句中文的语序与英语的语序习惯一致，其中涉及广为流传的"春节""春联"等表达，可按源语语序直译。而"福字"为中国文化特有，要准确说明张贴的是"福"这个汉字及其含义，则需要在直译的基础上进行一定增译。即译为"Chinese character 'fu', which means blessing"。

练习2

1. **原文**：It's doomed to be a white night because I'm laid off today and I'll be on the rocks soon.

参考译文：这注定是个不眠夜。因为今天我被解雇了，很快就会陷入经济困难。

解析：原文中"white night""on the rocks"均为英文固定短语或习语，如按字面意思直译，则会导致句意不通。因此需根据语境进行解释性翻译，译出短语的实际含义或寓意。此外还需按照中文习惯来调整语序，如将表示时间的词语 today 和 soon 提前。

2. **原文**：

A: We are one of the largest food suppliers in the UK. The purpose of my coming here today is to inquire about your purchase of frozen baked goods.

B: 你的消息真灵通。我们确实正准备为上海冷冻烘焙项目进行公开招标。

参考译文：

A: 我们是英国最大的食品供应商之一。我今天来的目的是咨询一下有关贵公司采购冷冻烘焙产品的事情。

B: You're very well-informed. We are indeed preparing an open tender for suppliers of the frozen baked goods in Shanghai.

解析："消息灵通"意译为"well-informed"即可达到意思对等的效果。此外，这两句话都需要根据目的语表达习惯对源语进行一定的语序调整，如在英文里，表示国家地名和时间的词在后，中文则常把它们提前。中译英时通常可先把主谓宾找出来并提前译出，再根据英语表达习惯确定定语、状语、补语等部分的位置。比如，"我们确实正准备为上海冷冻烘焙项目进行公开招标"这句话，按英语语序应先说主谓宾，即"我们确实正准备进行公开招标"，再补充说明是"为了上海冷冻烘焙项目"。"上海冷冻烘焙项目"如果直译为"Shanghai frozen baking project"，则未明确表达招标目的是采购服务还是产品。因此，英文应根据上下文对该招标项目进行解释性翻译，阐明是招冷冻烘焙食品供应商。

练习3

Text 1

原文：

今天，我非常荣幸站在这里，与各位一同探讨中国商务文化的重要性及其在现代国际商业中的应用。中国是一个拥有悠久历史和丰富文化传统的国家。在商业领域，中国的文化价值观对国际商务交易与合作具有重要影响力。//

其中之一就是"关系"，这是中国商务文化中的核心要素之一。在中国，我们认为建立和维护良好的人际关系至关重要，这不仅有助于商业合作，还有助于建立信任和长期合作关系。//

另一个重要的文化元素是"信任"。在中国商务环境中，建立信任关系需要时间和努力，但一旦建立起来，它将成为业务成功的基石。信任不仅仅是交易的

基础，更是商业伙伴关系的基础，涵盖了诚实、可靠和承诺的价值观。//

除了人际关系和信任，中国的商务文化还强调"谦虚"和"尊重"。在商业谈判中，谦虚的态度被视为一种优势，而不是弱点。尊重他人的观点和意见，展现出文化的开放性和尊重多样性的精神。//

当谈到谈判和交易时，中国的商务文化也注重"圆通"和"灵活"。在谈判过程中，双方通常会寻求妥协和双赢的解决方案，而不是强行推动自己的意愿。这种灵活性和顾全大局的态度有助于维持和谐的商业关系。//

总之，中国商务文化是一个深受历史和价值观影响的复杂体系。在国际商业环境中，了解并尊重这些文化元素对于有效的跨文化合作至关重要。通过建立良好的人际关系，树立信任，保持谦虚尊重、灵活圆通的态度，相信我们可以在跨文化商务中取得成功。谢谢大家！//

参考译文：

Today, I am greatly honored to stand here and discuss with you the significance of Chinese business culture and its application in modern international business. China is a country with a long history and rich cultural traditions. Within the realm of business, Chinese cultural values have a significant impact on international business transactions and cooperation. //

One such value is the concept of relationships, which is a core element of Chinese business culture. In China, we think it's essential to cultivate and maintain strong interpersonal relationships, not only for promoting business cooperation but also for fostering trust and long-term partnerships. //

Another crucial cultural element is trust. In China's business environment, building a foundation of trust takes time and effort. Yet once established, it becomes the bedrock of business success. Trust is not merely the basis of transactions, but also the foundation of business partnerships, encompassing values of honesty, reliability, and commitment. //

In addition to interpersonal relationships and trust, Chinese business culture places emphasis on humility and respect. In business negotiations, a humble manner is regarded as an advantage rather than a weakness. Respecting others' viewpoints and opinions showcases cultural openness and a spirit of respecting diversity. //

When it comes to negotiations and deals, Chinese business culture also lays stress on being tactful and flexible. Throughout negotiation processes, both parties often seek compromise and win-win solutions instead of forcefully pursuing their own agendas. This flexible and holistic approach contributes to maintaining harmonious business relationships. //

In conclusion, Chinese business culture is a complex system deeply influenced by history and values. In the international business landscape, understanding and respecting these cultural elements are essential for effective cross-cultural collaborations. Through building strong interpersonal relationships, establishing trust, and being humble, respectful, flexible and tactful in negotiations, I believe we can achieve success in cross-cultural business endeavors. Thank you! //

练习解析：

本段演讲中多为短句，和英文逻辑及句子结构相近，语体正式，总体可按源语语序进行直译，针对部分句子需按照英语表达习惯进行局部语序调整。其中提到多个商务文化元素，包括关系、信任、谦虚、尊重、灵活，都有对应的英文，且没有另外的文化内涵，直译即可。在此演讲的语境中的"圆通"带有褒义，是一种寻求双赢、顾全大局的态度，即应突出该词"灵活变通"的含义，可意译为英文中另一个意义和功能对等的褒义词"tactful"。此外，"顾全大局"可直译为"take the whole situation into account"，但联系本文语境来看，"顾全大局"修饰的是"态度"，且和"灵活性"并列，翻译为一个形容词会更适用，故简化意译为"holistic"，常搭配"approach"，表示全局观。

Text 2

原文：

In an increasingly interconnected world, effective communication transcends mere language proficiency. It covers an understanding of diverse cultures, nuances, and unspoken norms that shape interactions between businesses and individuals across borders. //

In today's dynamic business landscape, a company's ability to succeed is closely linked to its capacity to navigate cultural differences. This capacity extends far beyond the use of language alone. It hinges on an in-depth understanding of cultural dimensions such as power distance, individualism-collectivism, and uncertainty avoidance. //

For example, many Asian cultures prefer a high-context communication style, which requires attention to nuances often left unsaid. Embracing such nuances fosters trust and rapport, enabling us to build long-lasting partnerships. //

The concept of "saving face" is another cultural symbol that has profound implications for global business interactions. This notion, deeply rooted in many Asian cultures, dictates that public embarrassment or shame is to be avoided at all costs. To navigate this, it's essential to deliver feedback or criticism privately and constructively, allowing for constructive dialogue while preserving mutual respect. //

Understanding cultural connotations behind seemingly simple terms is crucial to avoid miscommunication. Take the term "deadline" as an example. In Western cultures, it signifies a firm cutoff point. // However, in cultures with a more flexible approach to time, like some Latin American cultures, deadlines might be perceived as more malleable. Mastery of such cultural nuances enables us to express expectations accurately, minimizing any potential misunderstandings. //

It's also essential to recognize that non-verbal communication plays a substantial role in cross-cultural contexts. Gestures, eye contact, and other body languages can convey as much, if not more, meaning than words themselves. //

For instance, while direct eye contact is a sign of confidence in many Western cultures, it can be interpreted as challenging or disrespectful in certain Asian cultures. As we delve into new markets and partnerships, cultivating this awareness will undoubtedly facilitate smoother interactions. //

第 7 单元　直译与意译

参考译文：

在一个日益互联的世界中，有效的交流已经超越了单纯的语言能力，它涵盖了如何理解不同文化、细微差别和潜规则，这些都影响着各国企业与个人之间的交流往来。//

在当今不断变化的商业环境中，一家公司的成功与其应对文化差异的能力紧密相连。这种能力远远超出了仅仅使用语言的范畴。它取决于深刻理解文化维度，如权力差距、个人主义与集体主义、规避不确定性。//

例如，高语境的沟通风格盛行于许多亚洲文化中，要求我们关注细微的差别，而且这些常常是没有明说的。接纳这样的细微差别可以促进信任和融洽，使我们能够建立持久的伙伴关系。//

"要面子"的观念是另一个文化符号，在全球商业交流中具有深远影响。这个观念在许多亚洲文化中根深蒂固，规定在公众场合出现尴尬或羞耻是无论如何要避免的。为此，提出反馈或批评时必须是私下且具有建设性，从而在进行建设性的对话的同时保持相互尊重。//

理解看似简单的术语背后的文化内涵对于避免误解至关重要。以"deadline"（截止时间）这个词为例。在西方文化中，它表示一个确定的截止时间点。// 然而，在一些文化中对待时间更加灵活，比如拉丁美洲的某些文化中，截止时间可能被视为是可变通的。掌握这种文化的细微差别使我们能够准确表达期望，从而最大限度地减少可能的误解。//

此外，我们还必须认识到非语言交流在跨文化背景中扮演着重要角色。手势、眼神接触等肢体语言可以传达与话语本身一样多甚至更多的意义。//

例如，直接的眼神接触在许多西方文化中表示自信，但在某些亚洲文化中，它可能被解读为挑战或不尊敬。随着我们深入探索新的市场和伙伴关系，培养这种意识无疑将有助于更加顺畅的交流往来。//

练习解析：

本段讲话涉及一些文化研究理论中的专有词汇，如"power distance""uncertainty avoidance""high-context"已在预习中标出，此类专有名词可采取直译，以确保专业准确性。此外，源语句子结构大多与中文接近，大体上可直译，但也需要根据中文语序习惯对一些定语、状语或补语的位置做调整。对于一些长句和从句，需要根据意群合理断句和调整语序。

比如，"It covers an understanding of diverse cultures, nuances, and unspoken norms that shape interactions between businesses and individuals across borders."此句中 that 后接的定语从句较长，如译为中文时调整语序将从句置于被修饰词即"diverse cultures, nuances, and unspoken norms"之前，会造成较大的翻译负担。故可以考虑顺句驱动，尽量不大规模地调整语序。此外，"unspoken norms"直译应为"不言而喻的规范或准则"，和中文的"潜规则"意义对等，因此可意译为"潜规则"更加简洁。

文中提到的"saving face"在亚洲文化中根深蒂固，直译为中文就是"保全面子"，但后面强调了这个观念的规定要求，"保全面子"更像是个动作而非观念，而且显得语气较弱，与这种强调更呼应且地道的翻译应当是"要面子"。在"deadlines might be perceived as more malleable"这句中，"malleable"直译应为"（材料）可塑的、（人）易受影响的"，但和修饰对象"截止时间"不搭配，故可根据上文提到"更加灵活对待时间"将其意译为"可变通的"。

练习 4

Dialogue 1

原文：

A: Hi, I'm Jessica Brown from the UK. I'm the manager in charge of the sales of solid wood flooring. Here's my business card. Nice to meet you!

B: 你好，布朗小姐，我叫李慧，你叫我李小姐就好。我公司预计向贵公司初步购取各类实木地板 250 万平方米。希望贵公司提供优质的实木地板材料以及合理的报价。

A: Combining the cost and market situation, our offer about solid wood flooring is \$50/m^2.

B: 这价格超出了我方的预算，希望贵公司所有种类的实木地板能给我们七折优惠。

A: Sorry. We cannot agree. Although there are a few companies whose price is lower than ours, the materials they used are very different. Overall, our company's products are the most cost-effective.

B: 贵公司产品的质量我们是放心的。你们在实木地板的维护方面一定花费了不少人力与资金。俗话说薄利多销，那么贵公司何不考虑呢？

A: These are some decoration cases of solid wood flooring done by our company before. I just want to emphasize the reliable quality assurance and advantages of our products, which are unmatched by other companies!

B: 贵公司的话相当有理。我们不如各退一步，我方加大订单量，贵公司可以将价格降低吗？

A: Yes, then all our products could be sold at 20% off.

B: 我同意。既然我们已经达成共识，那我们来讨论一下运输和支付问题。

A: Because of the long distance and the large order quantity, we will send them by sea freight. Do you accept partial shipment?

B: 可以的。这是我们起草的合同，一式两份，你可以看一下这里的条款明细。如果没有问题就可以签名了。我们还想问问大概什么时候能装船呢？

A: OK! Thank you for your support! I think we can ship the goods in June.

B: 好的，合作愉快！希望合同执行过程一切顺利。

A: Of course! I am confident that we will work well together and maintain a long-lasting partnership.

参考译文：

A: 你好，我是来自英国的 Jessica Brown，我是负责实木地板销售的经理，这是我的名片。很高兴认识你！

B: Hello, Miss Brown. I'm Li Hui, and you can just call me Miss Li. Our company expects to purchase 2.5 million square meters of solid wood flooring of various types from your company. We hope that your company will provide high-quality solid wood flooring materials as well as reasonable quotation.

A: 结合成本和市场形势，我方实木地板的报价是50美元/㎡。

B: Your price is beyond our budget. We hope your company could offer a 30% discount on all kinds of solid wood flooring.

A: 抱歉，我们无法答应这个条件。虽然有一些公司价格低于我们公司，但所用的材料有很大不同。总体来说，我们公司产品的性价比是最高的。

B: We believed that the quality of your company's products is assured. You must have spent a lot of manpower and money on the maintenance of the solid wood flooring. There is a saying of "small profits but quick turnover", so why don't you consider it?

A: 您看这些是我们公司以前做的一些实木地板的装修案例，我只是想向贵公司再次强调我们产品有可靠的质量保证与优势，这是其他公司所无法比拟的！

B: It's quite reasonable. Let's compromise with each other. If we increase the order quantity, could you reduce the prices?

A: 可以的，那我们全部产品可以八折销售。

B: Agree. Now that we've reached a consensus, let's talk about shipping and payment.

A: 由于距离较远且订单数量较大，我们会采用海运的方式。你们接受分批装运吗？

B: OK. This is the contract we drafted in duplicate, you can check the details of the terms. If there is no problem, you can sign it. We'd also like to ask when will you ship the goods?

A: 好的，谢谢你们的支持！我想我们大概可以在6月装船。

B: OK! Hope everything runs smoothly during the execution of the contract.

A: 当然！相信我们会合作愉快且长久。

练习解析：

此篇对话以短句为主，涉及行业词汇，应优先采取直译法。但部分语句可根据目的语的语法和语序习惯进行灵活调整，或意译为对等的目的语常用表达。比如其中"薄利多销"是常用俗语，可翻译为"small profit leads to large sales volume"，但少了源语中前后两字对仗的简洁风格，译为"small profits but quick turnover"，表示利润虽低但成交量多、资金周转快，则意义对等，与上文"已花费了不少人力资金"对应，且贴合源语的风格。

此外，最后一句"I am confident that we will work well together and maintain a long-lasting partnership."由于"work together"和"partnership"都表达合作关系，中文如果直译比较重复累赘，可意译为"相信我们会合作愉快且长久"，更加简洁。

Dialogue 2

原文：

A: 您好，很高兴见到您。我是广东省一家运动鞋销售公司的产品经理。

B: Hello, I am Evelyn. I heard that your company is planning to promote products. Can you give me more information?

A: 好的。感谢您的到来，请坐。我想为我们的产品做一个大型促销活动来提高产品的销量，您能给我们提供一个具体的方案吗？

B: Of course. We have investigated your products before and found that although the quality of your product is very good, the brand awareness is not strong. So I think you need an advertising campaign.

A: 做广告的成本很高吧，有什么好处吗？

B: There is an old saying in China, "Good wine needs no bush". But today the market competition is increasingly fierce, so "Good wine needs bush". It is not enough for an enterprise to merely have good quality and service. Only by combining with good advertisement can an enterprise remain invincible in the market.

A: 您说得很有道理。我们的产品质量很好，但就是销量不高。可能就是因为顾客对我们的产品不了解，不敢轻易购买。

B: You're right in thinking that way. Advertising does need a certain fee, but you may get more profit after advertising.

A: 我觉得这个想法值得一试。但是最后的决策要通过内部讨论决定。

B: I understand these processes. This is an advertising campaign plan that includes more details. I hope it can be adopted.

A: 好的，我们会尽快答复您。

B: Thank you. Looking forward to our next meeting!

A: 相信我们不久会见面。再见！

参考译文：

A: Hello, nice to meet you. I am the product manager of a sales company for sports shoes from Guangdong Province.

B: 您好，我是 Evelyn。我听说贵公司准备做产品促销活动。您能给我更多的信息吗？

A: OK! Thanks for being here. Please have a seat. We would like to do a large-scale promotion for our product to increase sales. Can you provide us with a specific plan?

B: 当然可以。我们之前调查过贵公司的产品，发现虽然贵司的产品质量很好，但品牌知名度不高。因此我觉得贵司需要做一个广告宣传活动。

A: Advertising can be quite costly, can't it? What are the benefits of it?

B: 中国有句古话："酒香不怕巷子深。"但如今市场竞争日益激烈,"酒香也怕巷子深"。企业仅有优质的产品和服务是不够的,只有配以良好的广告宣传,才能在市场上立于不败之地。

A: What you said is very reasonable. Our products are very good, but the sales volume is not high. It might be because customers aren't familiar with our products and are hesitant to purchase.

B: 您这样想就对了。广告是需要一定的费用,但是广告宣传后,贵公司可能得到更高的利润。

A: I think this is worth a try. But the final decision should be made through internal discussions.

B: 我理解这些流程。这是包含了更多的细节的广告活动方案。希望能够得到采纳。

A: I see. We will reply to you as soon as possible.

B: 谢谢。期待我们下一次见面!

A: I believe we will meet soon. Goodbye!

练习解析:

此篇对话同样以直译为主,部分语句可根据目的语的表达习惯进行灵活调整或增译减译。比如"It is not enough for an enterprise to merely have good quality and service. Only by combining with good advertisement can an enterprise remain invincible in the market."前一句是强调句,后一句是倒装句,在翻译时均需先将主语"企业"提前,"remain invincible"意思是保持不败,用中文中更地道的表达就是"立于不败之地"。此外,文中提到中国的古话"Good wine needs no bush",字面上的意思是说有好的红酒就不需用广告来吸引顾客,潜在的含义是好产品不用多做宣传,自然有人来买。联想后即可发现该句是中文中"酒香不怕巷子深"的意译版本。因此,译员应平时多查找积累各种习语俗语的直译和意译版本,一旦在口译实战中碰到便可结合语境自如应对。

Dialogue 3

原文:

A: 晚上好,我是 Vicky,是幸运玩偶公司的总监,我谨代表本公司欢迎你们的到来!

B: Hello, I'm Grace, the CEO of Happy Chocolate Company. It's my pleasure to visit your company.

A: 现在你们看到的这些都是我们公司已经推出的玩偶,目前在市场上非常受欢迎,这是因为我们公司致力于设计出大众喜闻乐见的玩偶。

B: They are indeed very exquisite, and I love your products! Your brand philosophy aligns with ours, as we also strive to create chocolates that meet customer demand with high quality and great taste.

A: 关于这次合作我们希望能推出一款新的联名产品,所以今天我们将主要讨论关于产品设计的大致方向。

B: Your dolls are highly popular in the Chinese market, and our chocolate brand leads in the industry. For this interdisciplinary collaboration, we plan to develop a series of new chocolate flavors that can be sold alongside your dolls. I believe this will generate a strong market response. If possible, we hope you can design relevant dolls to complement these chocolates.

A: 这是个好主意,你们优秀的产品加上我们新颖的玩偶进行捆绑销售,一加一大于二,实现共赢。你们如果有什么相关方面的要求请尽管提出来,我们一定积极配合。我司也一定会为我们的合作尽最大努力设计出受人欢迎的玩偶,请放心。

B: We will have dedicated personnel handle the details of our collaboration going forward. We are looking forward to this cooperation and hope for a successful partnership.

A: 合作愉快!我也非常期待我们的合作。

参考译文：

A: Good evening, I'm Vicky, director of Lucky Doll Company. On behalf of our company, I sincerely welcome you here!

B: 你好，我是 Happy Chocolate 公司的 CEO Grace，很荣幸能来参观你们的公司。

A: What you see here are the dolls our company has already launched, and they are currently very popular in the market. This is because our company is dedicated to designing dolls that appeal to people of all ages.

B: 确实非常精美，我很喜欢你们的产品！你们的品牌理念和我们一致，我们也致力于制造出贴合顾客需求，高品质、好口感的巧克力。

A: For this collaboration, we hope to launch a new co-branded product. So today, we mainly discuss the general direction for product design.

B: 贵公司的玩偶非常受到中国市场的欢迎，我们的巧克力品牌也是业内领先的，对于这一次跨领域合作，我们将研发一系列新口味的巧克力，搭配贵公司的玩偶进行组合销售，我想一定会带来非常好的市场反响。如果可以的话，希望你们也能设计出与这些巧克力搭配的相关玩偶。

A: That's a great idea, combining your excellent products with our innovative dolls for bundled sales can create a synergy effect and achieve win-win outcomes. If you have any specific requirements or requests in this regard, please feel free to let us know, and we will certainly do anything to help. We will also put our best efforts into designing popular dolls for our collaboration. You don't have to worry about that.

B: 后续的细节我们公司会安排专人对接，非常期待本次的合作，希望我们合作愉快。

A: Wish us a pleasant cooperation! I'm also looking forward to our cooperation.

练习解析：

　　原文多为短句，总体可按语序直译，其中部分需根据目的语表达习惯进行调整或增译减译。此外，部分词句的翻译为求简洁达意，可采取意译的方法。例如，"大众喜闻乐见的玩偶"是指受大众欢迎的玩偶，由于前文已提到玩偶受市场欢迎，这里应该强调其受众面广。如果直译为"dolls that people enjoy to hear and see"，并不合逻辑。意译为"dolls that appeal to people of all ages"，即可表达"受众面广"这一层含义。"一加一大于二"这一短语结合上文可理解为两个产品捆绑销售达到的效果会大于两个产品单独销售的效果叠加，从而实现共赢。这一现象在术语上也被称为协同效应。如果直译，不仅不合逻辑，也不能表达这一内涵，故应该采取意译，将其本质含义翻译出来，即"synergy effect"。

第 8 单元

公众演讲

虽然作为一名优秀的口译员，不应喧宾夺主、抢夺演讲者的风头，但是作为置身于公众视野的语言服务者，口译的输出本质上也属于公众演讲。因此提高公众演讲能力，也有助于提高口译输出的质量。

8.1 如何做好公众演讲

8.1.1 公众演讲注意事项

1. 关注听众

公众演讲者应从听众角度去思考和准备演讲的核心内容，即演讲内容对听众有什么价值，他们关心的是什么。优秀的公众演讲者应该是听众友好型的，能让听众兴致盎然、全神贯注，因为演讲内容包含着他们最感兴趣的东西。同时，在演讲前应评估听众对演讲主题的理解程度或专业水平，好提前准备演讲中要提供的背景知识以及演讲的专业性程度。最后，演讲者在演讲过程中应及时观察观众的反应，及时调整内容和节奏。

2. 眼神交流

与听众建立眼神互动有助于演讲者捕获反馈，进而判断是否需进一步解释以确保信息传递的清晰性。演讲者应确保视线遍及全场，而非局限于某一区域，从而使受众更有参与感。除了同传译员在固定位置（如同传箱）上，无须与观众互动，对于大部分口译员来说，在实践中都要面对听众。在口译时，除了参照笔记，还应注重与听众的眼神交往，及时感知其反馈。

3. 清晰发言

清晰发言在公众演讲中十分重要。除了发言内容本身的质量外，演讲者（包括口译员）声音本身的清晰度和语速也会影响听众的感受，声音应清晰且语速适中。学习者在练习时，一般内容不会有大问题，但是要么声音太小，要么因为紧张讲得太快，又或是拿着麦克风不停晃动导致音质很差。如果因此让听众怀疑你的专业水平，质疑你的翻译内容，那就太可惜了。

另外，要避免出现过多的填充词（filler words），如"我觉得""是吧""所以""literally""you know""well""um""ah"等。

4. 开头与结尾

引人入胜的开场往往能引起听众的兴趣，惊人的数据、个人轶事、名人语录，都可以作为开场内容吸引听众。用"吸睛点"完美收尾也能让听众对你的演讲印象深刻。"吸睛点"可以是一个故事、一个比喻或对未来的畅想，最好与演讲前面部分提及的一些内容首尾呼应。

5. 善用动作

正确使用肢体语言可以让公众演讲更加生动，手势有助于强调重点或引导受众的注意力。某些动词，如"游泳"或"飞翔"，可以通过面部和手部表达呈现其意象。然而，需谨防因紧张产生的无意动作。对口译员而言，不宜模仿讲者的肢体动作，尤其是讲者在紧张场合表现出的强烈情绪。译员应仅确切传达讲者的含义和情感，而非具体动作。

8.1.2　公众演讲练习与准备

1. 录音录像

你可以请同学、朋友或家人在你演讲后提供反馈，也可以进行自我评估。你也可以在预演排练时录制自己的表现，在录像中发现问题，如过多的填充词、无意义的手势、眼神飘忽不定等。平常进行口译练习时也可录音，通过复听来发现错误并加以改进。

2. 模拟练习

提前模拟演练，结合上一条建议，确定是否已经连贯且清晰地组织了信息。如果有准备 PPT，可以利用"排练计时"功能，看看自己在每一页幻灯片上的用时。同时，切记在公众演讲时要面向观众，不要一直盯着屏幕。

3. 持续学习

不断学习和积累知识，了解各类专业领域的词汇和用语。持续提高自身的语言能力和专业知识，有助于在公众演讲及口译中更好地表现。通过持续练习，逐步提高自己的技能水平。

在任何公众场合下的演讲，最重要的一点就是要坚定信念，你的信念决定你的表现，良好的信念能提升自信，保持自信和耐心，才能不断进步，并逐步提高自己的公众演讲技能水平。

8.2 公众演讲口译

在商务场合，如在商务洽谈中，双方常常会在一开始介绍自己的企业、部门等情况，这其实也属于公众演讲的类型。译员要快速准确地理解和转换语言，将演讲者的内容传达给听众。以下几点建议可以帮助译员在公众演讲口译中取得良好的效果：

8.2.1 准备工作

在公众演讲之前，尽可能获取演讲稿或相关资料，提前熟悉演讲主题和内容。如果在工作前能与演讲者进行交谈，就可以更好地了解演讲者的语音、用语习惯和语速，从而更好地熟悉演讲者的表达风格。

8.2.2 听力训练

进行大量的听力练习，提高对不同口音、语速和语调的适应能力。通过听新闻、演讲和讲座等内容，训练自己快速捕捉信息和转换语言的能力。

8.2.3 笔记和记忆

由于公众演讲的场合不一定适合拿着笔记本做笔记，译员往往会站在演讲者旁边，有时还需要拿麦克风。因此，要尽量减少对笔记的依赖，培养记忆力，使口译更加流畅。如果可以做笔记，应采用简洁的笔记和符号来帮助捕捉关键信息，但不可完全依赖笔记。

8.2.4 自信和流利

保持自信，尽量做到流利表达。即使遇到困难的内容，也要冷静处理，寻找最合适的表达方式，确保传达的准确性。尤其在商务谈判中，译员和讲者一样需要优良的心理素质。保持自信冷静、头脑清晰，这是展现实力、顺畅沟通并取得成功的重要条件。

8.2.5 小组练习

学习者可以与其他同学一起进行小组练习，模拟公众演讲场景，相互评估和提供反馈，共同进步。

8.3 口译练习

练习 1

Text 1

请听录音，这是一段探讨全球化对商务环境影响的演讲。录音已分割为多个语段，请在提示音后暂停录音并开始口译。练习后，先对照参考译文查缺补漏，再以公众演讲的形式将译文通读一遍，同时注意语音语调和肢体语言。

词汇预习

信息和技术的传播	the dissemination of information and technology
敏锐洞察	have a keen insight into
多元化的人才	diverse talents
文化培训项目	cultural training programs
敏捷和适应性	agility and adaptability

Text 2

请听录音,这是一段介绍有效商务沟通的重要性的演讲,请先预习词汇。录音已分割为多个语段,请在提示音后暂停录音并开始口译。

词汇预习

利益相关者	stakeholders
文化细微差别	cultural nuances
文化敏感性	cultural sensitivity
利用	leverage

练习 2

Dialogue 1

在对话口译练习中,你们可以组成四人小组进行练习,两人为讲者,两人为译员。当然,你也可以通过扫码进行自主练习,在提示音后进行口译。练习中注意运用公众演讲技巧,保持合适的语音语调和眼神交流。

词汇预习

广交会	China Import and Export Fair
性价比高的	cost-effective
到岸价	CIF (cost, insurance and freight)
以……为准	be subject to...

Dialogue 2

四人小组对话口译练习，可互换讲者和译员角色。同样，你也可以进行自主练习。

词汇预习

专业配件	professional accessories
技术检验及考核	technical inspection and assessment
概况，简介	profile
毛利润	gross margin

Dialogue 3

四人小组对话口译练习，自选讲者和译员角色。同样，你也可以进行自主练习。

词汇预习

深圳惠丰钢铁制造	Shenzhen Huifeng Steel Manufacturing
钢板	steel plates
汽车供应商	automotive supplier
初步报价	initial quote

模拟口译练习

请以 4～6 人为一组，自选商务主题，自定译员及讲者。形式可以为访谈、演讲、新闻发布会等。

8.4 练习原文、译文

练习1

Text 1

原文:

尊敬的各位嘉宾,女士们,先生们,

非常感谢大家出席今天的会议。我很荣幸有机会在此向大家分享有关全球化对商务环境的影响。//

全球化是当今世界不可忽视的重要趋势。它极大地改变了商业环境,为企业带来了新的机遇和挑战。首先,全球化打破了国界,扩大了市场的规模和范围。企业可以进入更广阔的市场,拓展业务,增加收入。// 其次,全球化加速了信息和技术的传播,使企业可以更快地获取和分享最新的市场动态和竞争信息。然而,全球化也带来了激烈的竞争和市场不确定性。企业需要更敏锐地洞察市场变化,灵活调整战略,并建立全球化的合作伙伴关系。//

对于企业而言,理解全球化趋势和适应商务环境的变化至关重要。首先,企业需要投资于多元化的人才和文化培训项目,以提高跨文化交际能力和团队协作能力。其次,积极采纳新技术和数字化工具,提高业务效率和竞争力。最后,建立稳固的合作网络,与全球合作伙伴分享资源和信息,共同应对全球化带来的机遇和挑战。//

总结而言,全球化对商务环境产生了深远的影响。它为企业带来了广阔的市场和增长机会,同时也要求企业保持敏捷和适应性。只有通过不断学习和适应,企业才能在全球化时代取得成功。

谢谢大家的聆听。//

参考译文:

Distinguished guests, Ladies and gentlemen,

Thank you very much for attending today's conference. I am honored to have the opportunity to be here and share with you the impact of globalization on the business environment. //

Globalization is an undeniable and significant trend in today's world. It has greatly transformed the business landscape, bringing both new opportunities and challenges for companies. Firstly, globalization has broken down barriers and expanded the scale and scope of markets. Companies can tap into broader markets, expand their businesses, and boost revenue. // Secondly, globalization has accelerated the dissemination of information and technology, enabling companies to access and share the latest market trends and competitive information more quickly. However, globalization has also brought fierce competition and market uncertainty. Companies need to have a keen insight into market changes, adjust their strategies flexibly, and establish global partnerships. //

It's vital for companies to understand globalization trends and adapt to the evolving business environment. First, companies should invest in diverse talents and cultural training programs to enhance their cross-cultural communication and teamwork abilities. Second, they should actively adopt new technologies and digital tools to improve business efficiency and competitiveness. Lastly, forging robust networks of collaboration and sharing resources and information with international partners to jointly address the opportunities and challenges brought by globalization. //

In conclusion, globalization has had a profound impact on the business environment. It brings vast markets and growth opportunities for companies while demanding agility and adaptability. Only through continuous learning and adaptation can companies achieve success in the era of globalization.

Thank you for your attention. //

Text 2

原文：

Distinguished guests, ladies and gentlemen,

Thank you all for being here today. I am honored to have the opportunity to speak to you about the importance of effective business communication. //

In today's fast-paced and interconnected world, effective communication is crucial for the success of any business. Clear and concise communication helps to build strong relationships, enhances teamwork, and drives productivity. It is the foundation for effective collaboration, both within the organization and with external stakeholders. //

First, effective business communication ensures that everyone within the organization is on the same page. By conveying information accurately and efficiently, it minimizes misunderstandings, reduces errors, and fosters a shared understanding of goals and expectations. It facilitates the smooth flow of information, enabling timely decision-making and problem-solving. //

Furthermore, effective communication plays a vital role in building strong relationships with clients, customers, and partners. It enables businesses to understand their needs, address their concerns, and provide excellent customer service. Effective communication also helps to negotiate contracts, resolve conflicts, and maintain long-term partnerships based on trust and mutual understanding. //

In today's global business landscape, cross-cultural communication is becoming increasingly important. Businesses operate in diverse cultural environments, and effective intercultural communication is essential for success. Understanding cultural nuances, adapting communication styles, and demonstrating cultural sensitivity are critical to building trust and fostering successful collaborations across borders. //

To enhance business communication, organizations should prioritize training programs centered on effective communication skills. These programs should cover various aspects such as active listening, clear and concise writing, public speaking, and nonverbal communication. Additionally, leveraging technology tools and platforms can facilitate efficient communication, particularly in a remote or global work environment. //

In conclusion, effective business communication is the key to success in today's dynamic and competitive business world. By fostering clear, concise, and culturally sensitive communication practices, organizations can enhance productivity, build strong relationships, and achieve their goals.

Thank you for your attention. //

参考译文：

尊敬的嘉宾，女士们，先生们，

非常感谢大家今天的光临。我很荣幸有机会向大家介绍有效商务沟通的重要性。//

在当今快节奏、紧密相连的世界中，有效沟通对任何企业的成功至关重要。清晰简明的沟通有助于建立牢固的关系，增强团队合作，并推动生产力。它是有效合作的基础，无论是组织内部还是与外部的利益相关者之间的合作。//

首先，有效商务沟通确保组织内的每个人都在同一起跑线上。通过准确高效地传达信息，它减少了误解和错误，并促进了对目标和期望的共同理解。它也促进了信息的流畅传递，使得及时决策和解决问题成为可能。//

此外，有效沟通在与客户、顾客和合作伙伴建立牢固关系方面起着至关重要的作用。它使企业能够了解他们的需求，解决他们的关切，并提供卓越的客户服务。有效沟通还有助于合同谈判、解决冲突，并基于信任和相互理解建立长期合作伙伴关系。//

在当今全球商业环境中，跨文化沟通变得越来越重要。企业在多元文化环境中运营，有效的跨文化沟通对于成功至关重要。理解文化细微差别，适应沟通风格，表现出文化敏感性，对于在跨境合作中建立信任和促成成功至关重要。//

为了提升商务沟通能力，各组织应该投资专注于有效沟通技巧的培训项目。这些培训项目应涵盖积极倾听、清晰简明的书面表达、公共演讲和非语言沟通等各个方面。此外，在远程或全球工作环境中，利用技术工具和平台可以促进高效沟通。//

总之，在当今充满活力和竞争的商业世界中，有效商务沟通是取得成功的关键。通过促进清晰、简明和具有文化敏感性的沟通，组织可以提高生产力，建立牢固的关系，并实现目标。

谢谢大家的关注。//

练习 2

Dialogue 1

原文：

A: 欢迎光临广交会。我是深圳开心鞋业有限公司销售部的经理。请问有什么可以帮到您呢？

B: Hello, I am Miss Smith, the head of a retail company in Singapore, mainly selling shoes. We are very interested in your shoes and would like to inquire about the prices. If the price is right, we can proceed with the business immediately.

A: 我相信我们的价格是具有市场竞争力的。我们的价格一直十分稳定，相较于其他的同类产品，我们是性价比更高的选择。

B: In that case, that would be great. My business is still in the infancy stage and I hope to find a partner to achieve mutual benefit.

A: 我们也是这么希望的。史密斯小姐，您希望具体了解哪个种类的鞋子呢？

B: Sneakers are the best sellers in our store, so we'd like to know the lowest CIF Singapore for sneakers.

A: 这是我们价目表。价格以我们最后签订的为准。

B: I checked the price list. Since we will place a large order, can you give us some discount?

A: 如果你们的订单量足够大的话，我们愿意降价3%。

B: OK, let's sign the contract.

A: 这里是我们的合同，本合同一式两份，双方各执一份。请您确认无误后，在最后一页签字。

B: OK. I'm very delighted to cooperate with your company.

A: 谢谢。

参考译文：

A: Welcome to China Import and Export Fair. I'm the sales manager at Shenzhen Happy Shoes Co., Ltd. How can I help you?

B: 你好，我是史密斯小姐，新加坡的一个零售公司的负责人，主要以销售鞋子为主。我们对你们生产的鞋子非常感兴趣，想要了解一下鞋子的价格。如果价格合适的话，我们可以马上做这笔生意。

A: I believe our prices are competitive in the market. Compared with other similar products, we have stable prices and must be a more cost-effective choice.

B: 既然如此，那就太好了。我的事业还处于起步阶段，希望能找到一个能够互利共赢的合作伙伴。

A: That's what we hope. What kind of shoes would you like to know specifically, Miss Smith?

B: 在我们的商店里，运动鞋的销量是最高的，所以我们想了解运动鞋到新加坡的最低到岸价。

A: Here is our price list. The price is subject to the contract.

B: 我看了一下这个价目表，因为我们所需要的订单量比较大，请问你们可以给一些折扣吗？

A: If your order is large enough, we are willing to reduce our price by 3%.

B: 好的，那我们来签合同吧！

A: Here is our contract. It is done in duplicate, with each party holding one copy. Please sign on the last page after you confirm it.

B: 好的。非常高兴能与贵公司合作。

A: Thank you.

Dialogue 2

原文：

A: 晚上好，Nancy 女士。

B: Good evening, Ms. Wang.

A: 今天来和您进行这场会议是为了与贵公司就合作事宜进行洽谈，希望今天能有一个愉快的结果。

B: We're also pleased to discuss potential cooperation with your company and hope to reach an agreement today.

A: 我方目前已对贵公司的产品进行了初步了解，但功能方面尚不清晰，贵公司可否为我们再讲讲？

B: Of course, we have already prepared a detailed introduction of the products for you and my colleague Belinda will explain it to you.

C: Our products boast 34 functions of their types on the market and introduced functional innovation in four aspects such as the combination of software and hardware. The professional accessories required for each function have passed our technical inspection and assessment, all of which have reached excellent standards. It's absolutely right to choose our products. I will ask our secretary to send the product profile to your company's mailbox, so you can check out the details.

A: 这样看来，产品功能的确很齐全，但是价格还有点问题。

B: What concerns do you have about the price? Do you find it too high?

A: 是的。贵公司的报价经过我方仔细地考虑与讨论，一致认为报价过高。以长期合作的角度来看希望贵方再考虑一下，给出我方可以接受的报价。

B: Then what do you think?

A: 我方认为价格可以降低20%，毕竟现在市场行情不太好。

B: We can adjust the price, but a 20% reduction is too much. This would significantly impact our gross margin. The price of the products also matches with the quality. We can only accept a discount of 8%.

A: 贵公司的产品质量的确没得说。这也是我们选择贵公司的原因，但现在受国际形势的影响我们不是很好做，在价格这方面我认为最少要降价10%。

B: Fine, after full consideration, we think 10% is acceptable. In the interest of long-term collaboration, we can agree to a 10% discount. We look forward to a fruitful partnership.

A: 好，合作愉快。

参考译文：

A: Good evening, Ms. Nancy.

B: 晚上好，王女士。

A: I'm here to have this meeting with you to discuss potential cooperation with your company. I hope we can come to a favorable agreement today.

B: 我方也很乐意与贵公司进行谈判，希望今天我们能达成交易。

A: At present, we have a preliminary understanding of your company's products, but we don't know about the function clearly yet. Can you tell us more about it?

B: 当然，我们已经事先为贵公司准备了详细的产品介绍，我的同事 Belinda 将会为您进行讲解。

C: 关于我们的产品，它集合了市面上现有同类产品的 34 种功能，并做了如软硬件结合等四个方面的功能创新。与此同时，每个功能所需的专业配件都通过了我们的技术检验及考核，全部达到了优秀的标准，所以选择我们的产品绝对是不二选择。回头我让我们的秘书将这份产品简介发到贵公司的邮箱，您可以查看更多细节。

A: In this way, the products indeed have complete functions, but there is still a problem with the price.

B: 价格方面是哪里的问题呢？是报价过高吗？

A: Yes, after careful consideration and discussion of your company's quotation, we all agree that it is too high. From the perspective of long-term cooperation, I hope you can reconsider and give us an acceptable quotation.

B: 那您觉得多少合适？

A: We think the price can be reduced by 20%. After all, the market is not optimistic now.

B: 我们可以降低价格，但 20% 太多了，这会大大削减我们的毛利润。而且我们的质量与产品的价格是相匹配的。我们可以接受 8% 的降价。

A: The quality of your company's products is unquestionable and that's the reason why we choose your company. However, our business has been greatly affected by the international situation. I think the price should be reduced by at least 10%.

B: 好的，经过我方充分思考，我方认为 10% 的降价是可以接受的。为了我们长久的合作，那就降价 10% 吧。祝我们合作愉快！

A: Hope we will have good cooperation.

Dialogue 3

原文：

A: 早上好，Smith 先生。作为深圳惠丰钢铁制造的代表，我非常荣幸能与您就钢板的定价进行讨论。我们对与纽约汽车合作感到非常期待，希望能够建立一种稳定而互利的合作关系。

B: Good morning, Mr. Li. I'm also looking forward to our collaboration. Products from Huifeng Steel Manufacturing have always been highly regarded by us. Before we finalize the price, we need to take into account our budget and the market conditions.

A: 我们非常理解。作为贵公司的供应商，我们希望能为您提供一个具有竞争力的价格，同时也要保障我们的利润。我们的初步报价是每吨 1000 美元。

B: Thank you for your quote, Mr. Li. However, I must point out that we have seen some competitors offering lower prices in the market. We hope to work towards a more competitive price with you.

A: 作为一家有远见的制造商，我们愿意在价格上做出一些让步。我们可以将价格调整为每吨 950 美元。这已经是我们的底线了。

B: Thank you for your concession, Mr. Li. However, I must say that we still hope to further reduce the price to meet our budget. Our upper limit is $900 per ton.

A: 我完全理解您的考虑，Smith 先生。虽然这会对我们的利润造成一些影响，但考虑到我们追求长期友好合作的愿望，我们愿意接受每吨 925 美元的价格。

B: Mr. Li, thank you for your understanding. I believe the price of $925 per ton is acceptable. We are eager to establish a long-term partnership with you and look forward to exploring further collaboration opportunities in future transactions.

A: 非常感谢您的合作，Smith 先生。我们深感荣幸能与纽约汽车建立合作关系。我们将确保为您提供高质量的钢板产品和卓越的服务，满足您的需求。

B: I look forward to this collaboration opportunity as well, Mr. Li. Thank you for your efforts and willingness to compromise. I believe this will be a successful partnership.

参考译文：

A: Good morning, Mr. Smith. As the representative of Shenzhen Huifeng Steel Manufacturing, it is my great honor to discuss the pricing for steel plates with you. We are looking forward to collaborating with the New York Automotive and aim to establish a stable and mutually beneficial partnership.

B: 早上好，李先生。我也很期待与您的合作。惠丰钢铁制造的产品一直以来都备受我们的青睐。在最终确定价格之前，我们需要考虑我们的预算和市场形势。

A: We completely understand. As your supplier, we aim to provide you with a competitive price while ensuring our profitability. Our initial quote is $1,000 per ton.

B: 感谢您的报价，李先生。然而，我必须指出，我们在市场上看到了一些竞争对手提供的更低价格。我们希望能与您达成一个更具竞争力的价格。

A: As a forward-thinking manufacturer, we are willing to make some concessions on the price. We can adjust the price to $950 per ton. This is already our bottom line.

B: 感谢您的让步，李先生。但是我必须说，我们仍然希望能够进一步降低价格以满足我们的预算。我们的上限是每吨 900 美元。

A: I completely understand your considerations, Mr. Smith. While this may have some impact on our profitability, considering our desire for a long-term, friendly cooperation, we are willing to accept the price of $925 per ton.

B: 李先生，感谢您的理解。我也认为 925 美元是可接受的价格。我们愿意与您建立长期的合作关系，并期待在未来的交易中进一步探索合作机会。

A: Thank you very much for your cooperation, Mr. Smith. We are honored to establish a partnership with the New York Automotive. We will ensure to provide you with high-quality steel plate products and excellent service to meet your needs.

B: 我也很期待这次合作机会，李先生。感谢您的付出和让步。我相信这会是一次成功的合作。